RADIO HEAVEN

One Woman's Journey to Grace

by Dr. Sam Collins

CONTENTS

FOREWORD 5

CHAPTER 1   This Is Goodbye 9

CHAPTER 2   Council Estate Kid 25

CHAPTER 3   Bully Trouble.......................................33

CHAPTER 4   The Iron Lady 40

CHAPTER 5   Anything A Boy Can Do 45

CHAPTER 6   Que Sera Sera 56

CHAPTER 7   Fail Is Not a Four-Letter Word 66

CHAPTER 8   Poker Face 82

CHAPTER 9   The Unhappiest Day of My Life............94

CHAPTER 10   Nutty Professor 105

CHAPTER 11   The Ordeal 113

CHAPTER 12   Desperately 118

CHAPTER 13   California Dreamin' 130

CHAPTER 14   The Queen & I 137

CHAPTER 15   One O'clock Deadline.......................147

CHAPTER 16   Earthquake Jake & Halloween Charlie 159

CHAPTER 17   Getting M.A.D....................................169

CHAPTER 18   Baby Room to Board Room...............175

CHAPTER 19   A Lesson in Resilience.......................180

CHAPTER 20   Gas & Brakes.....................................187

CHAPTER 21   The Journey to Grace 199

ABOUT THE AUTHOR....................................... 215

FOREWORD

Reading this book will undoubtedly be one of your 'Radio Heaven' moments. I know it is for me. I have just finished reading it, with tears streaming down my face, love in my heart, inspiration in my soul and a fire in my belly that will make me follow my dreams.

I met Sam in 2010 at an Aspire Foundation event. As you will read in this wonderful book, Sam set up the Aspire Foundation as a result of learning about Women for Women International and our work to empower women survivors of war.

You know how there are people in your life who shape you and when you look back, they are there on one of the chairs reserved for VIPs in your life? Sam is one of them. Not only has she helped me to believe in myself, to turn my voice into an authentic roar, but she has also supported me professionally to be the best Executive Director I can be for Women for Women International. Sam was for me one of the supporters that she talks about in her book, someone who comes to the rescue when you really need them.

'Radio Heaven' tells the beautiful story of Sam, how she overcame obstacles, how "failure is an excellent stepping-stone to success," and how she learned to believe in herself and to allow herself to dream, really tune in with what is important to her, work hard and develop the resilience to make her dreams come true.

One important aspect Sam explores is how you can learn and see the positive even in the harshest circumstances. It is often the challenges we experience in life that are the source of the best developments for us.

Particularly inspiring and something that really resonated with me is her reflection on being bullied as a child. It formed in her a strong resolve to put her head above the parapet, as she says, "the world needs people to put their head above the parapet and say, "you are not allowed to do that."" As readers we learn how Sam stands up for her own dreams but also how she does this to advocate for others.

As her journey to find Grace begins, we learn about her passion for family and her desire to make a difference at the same time. She embarks on the international adoption of a little girl in DR Congo, a country I know well, internationally infamous for its conflicts and violence against women and girls. I applaud her bravery and commitment to diversity, race and an orphan crisis that needs both a short term and long term sustainable solution to change.

Sam is the strongest advocate for women's leadership I know. She empowers you to follow your instincts and behave in a way that feels right for you. By sharing her own journey, she reflects on the challenges but concludes: "Women are often told we're too emotional or too fluffy when listening to our gut instincts. I say it's the most important thing going, and our homes and workplaces need more of it, not less."

Sam bares her soul, 'warts and all' and asks you to define your dream. And with that this becomes the most powerful book I have read. It's a great read, it has a fantastic love story, a strong female character, but it also talks directly to the reader, disarming you from any fears or constraints, inviting you to be honest with yourself, because Sam is being so honest with you.

I invite you to really get to know Sam. She is an incredible woman, who has achieved so much—not least receiving recognition from the Queen and running a successful business, while building a family at the same time. But Sam is also real and an ordinary woman who purposefully avoids putting herself on a pedestal. She is definitely not a saint or into self-sacrifice and also not Superwoman coming to the rescue. Yet, she is incredible, but in a way that won't make you feel like saying, "I can't do that"—instead you will feel, "I am going to do it!"

And that is why this is the most powerful book I have ever read!

Brita Fernandez Schmidt

Executive Director

Women for Women International

CHAPTER 1

This Is Goodbye

We drove to the funeral with my dad on a cold November day in Essex. It was 1992 and I was a student in my final year of university in Liverpool. I turned on the radio to try and brighten up the uncomfortable silence of the car ride. When Always Look On the Bright Side of Life by Monty Python came on, I felt goose bumps and turned around in my seat to look at my younger sister, Emma.

She smiled a little for the first time in days and whispered, "Radio Heaven," and we both burst into tears again, knowing Mum was having the last laugh as usual.

"Always look on the bright side of life...

Life's a piece of shit,

When you look at it.

Life's a laugh and death's a joke, it's true.

You'll see it's all a show.

Keep 'em laughing as you go.

Just remember that the last laugh is on you.

And always look on the bright side of life...

(Come on guys, cheer up!)"

Mum had always believed in something she called "Radio Heaven," when a song came on the air that contained a special message for you. I guess she wanted to cheer us all up now. Dad switched the radio off, his face was red as he bit his lip.

#

Back when I was a teenager, Mum's power-suits became more powerful the further she rose up the corporate ladder. She had less time, too, and different priorities, spending long hours at work. Before she rejoined the workforce, she would always have dinner ready when my dad arrived home from his job, but it had become impossible with her blossoming career in finance and problems in their marriage were ever-growing.

When I turned eighteen, a few months away from going to university in Liverpool, Mum confided in me that she had met someone else and wanted to leave Dad. I listened and tried to be objective, encouraging her to think it through. It would be another year before my parents separated. When it finally happened, my mum left and my dad stayed. Two weeks after she left him, he had a girlfriend too, with same name as my mum—Gillian, but spelled with a J.

I was glad to be in my second year of university, building my own life, a little removed from the drama. Emma stayed with Mum; she didn't want to live with Dad when the new Jillian moved in.

Soon we discovered something new about my mum. We were surprised to learn that she had harbored a secret dream all her life, something she sacrificed for the sake of marriage and children, something adventurous. She wanted to live in Australia. Only days after the ink dried on the settlement, which almost broke my dad financially, she bought a ticket to Sydney and left to find a place for her and Emma.

I was surprised, but impressed. I knew my mum was an outgoing person, but she had never been daring, with the solitary exception of being married outside the family religion. She had never before hinted to me about this adventurous side, but I was thrilled to learn. After all, we now had something in common. I had discovered the empowerment of building my own life at school, and creating my own adventures, so I understood her excitement completely.

How I envied their move! When you grow up in the South of England, the beaches of Australia appear glamorous and idyllic. I missed my family being all together, of course, but I was so happy for my mum. She was making her dreams come true and talking with excitement and anticipation for the future.

Except, the thing about being halfway around the world is that it's easy to hide the truth. Behind my mum's cheery letters, happy phone calls, and beautiful beach photos, she was hiding a desperate secret. She had done so well in England and was confident of finding a similar career in Sydney, but came up short. The money dwindled fast and she panicked. She had embarked on her dream with no fallback plan, no means to stay on in this distant country without a steady income to sustain her, and no family to rely on back home in case she needed help. Her rosy dream had wilted.

Nine months after the dramatic departure, she and Emma came back to England completely broke. My dad still lived in the same house, worked the same job, and came home to a Jillian and supper on the table. It seemed like nothing much had changed for him. But everything had changed for my mum. She was broke, in debt, jobless, and, to top it off, the only affordable place she could find to rent was back on the low-income council estate where I had grown up.

Selfishly, I was glad to have them back, and I visited from Liverpool every spare moment as I had missed them both so much. When I was with them it felt a lot like when we were kids, with my mum at home and my dad away at work, and even though we had no money, we always had fun together.

Mum eventually found a new job doing accounts for a small company in Aldershot and seemed back in her element. She met a man named Craig and they started dating seriously. From my view, everything seemed back on track for her.

One university break, I took a quick trip down to visit Mum and Craig for a much needed rest. We were watching TV one evening and Mum said, "You know, I was watching this program the other day where this man was so depressed, he walked down to his shed in the back of his garden and shot himself."

"That's awful," I said. "Why on earth would you tell me that? I don't want to talk about that." I quickly dismissed the comment. Mum changed the subject and we finished the night with more TV and chatting. I forgot all about it.

A few days later we were sitting talking about something when she suddenly interrupted, "Hey, I've a great idea! Let's buy a chocolate cake and eat the whole thing."

At first I thought this a little odd. Mum always watched what she ate because her weight yo-yoed up and down most of her life. The women in our family struggled with weight, so it was a well-travelled subject in the household. But what is life if you can't do something fun every now and then?

"Well, we've certainly never done that before," I said with a shrug. "Let's do it."

We demolished the giant cake together. It was delicious, it was fun, and what's more I was starting to love her new spontaneity. As for the few extra pounds, we'll live to diet another day!

At the end of my weekend visit Mum drove me back to Farnborough train station in her blue Mini Cooper and waited with me on the platform.

"I'll see you in three weeks," she said, as the train rounded the corner.

"You will?"

"Yes, I'm going to drive up and leave the car with so you can use it for a little while. I'm not going to need it."

"Brilliant!" I said. We hugged and she kissed me, and I boarded the train, waving goodbye from the window. She stood and waved back, smiling and blowing kisses. I thought she looked so young, wearing a light blue denim jacket with white stripes, blue jeans, and a t-shirt.

On the train ride back to Liverpool, I planned the trip in my mind. Mum looked like a college kid, so I giggled a little when I imagined taking her out for drinks at the student union, boys mistaking her for my friend and asking her to dance or chatting her up. I giggled, anticipating the fun I'd have showing her off.

I love my mum so much, I thought. I can't wait to see her.

But that was the last time I would see her alive.

Three weeks later, early in the evening, I sat in the student union trying to have a drink with my friends. I felt weird. I don't know how else to describe it—weird, like something was about to happen. I had never felt anything like it before. I couldn't shake it and I was tired from study, anyway. I took the fifteen-minute walk back to my dorm thinking I needed to go to bed. When I opened the door my phone was already ringing. It was Emma, frantic.

"We can't find Mum," she said. "We can't find her."

"What do you mean you can't find her?"

"She's been missing a whole day. We've been looking for her and we can't find her."

"Emma, it's okay," I said, realizing the mistake, "that's because she's driving up here. She told me she was going to come up a couple of weeks ago and she's probably on her way now. I mean, I'm surprised she didn't say so, but I'm sure she's okay. You know how she is."

Surely Mum was on her way, maybe intercepted by some adventure. Since returning from Sydney, her adventurous streak had gained further notoriety. Once, after a long drive, she stopped at a hotel to rest and, down in the pub, she struck up a conversation with some young men from Norway, only to find out it was the band members from A-ha, my favorite boy band in school, and boy, was I jealous.

"She's probably having some deep conversation with A-ha," I said. "I'll call you when she gets here." Since cell phones weren't yet on the scene, there was no other way to reach her, we would just have to wait.

As I hung up the phone, I consciously shoved back a feeling that something was terribly wrong. My logical brain wouldn't allow it—once logic kicks in, it can't fathom anything bad happening, it makes excuses and it justifies—but my gut told me otherwise. I tried to get some sleep, but my body refused.

Emma called back hours later. She sounded different this time, monotone and high-pitched at the same time. "Sam, the police have been here," she said. "They told us they've found a woman's body in a hotel room in London." She stopped talking for a moment. "They think it's Mum." She started to sob. "They think she killed herself."

In the movies when people hear bad news they sort of collapse. All the energy to stand drains out of them and their body flops to the floor in shock. That's what happened to me. I slumped to my knees, barely clinging to the phone, stunned. The earth slowed and then stopped. I couldn't breathe. My view of the world changed instantly.

"It can't be her, Emma," I said, insisting it more than believing it. "It's not her. Don't worry, it can't be her." I tried to convince us both, repeating the words over and over. "I'll get on the first train. I'm coming."

I took the first possible train early the next day. My boyfriend, Christopher, came with me for support. We met my dad, Craig, and Emma at Euston station in rush hour—all of us falling into each other's arms, all of us in a weird, nightmarish daze. Early morning commuters rushed by, staring at us as we cried together.

We drove to Westminster Central police station. At first, they told us some hopeful news. They thought they were wrong and it might not be her after all. Our hopes rose. My theory of her being off somewhere, having fun, would prove true. I was sure of it. The police told us to wait, so we waited.

A short while later a policewoman approached us. She sat next to me in the busy police station waiting room, looked around at us all and said, "I'm very sorry to have to tell you that we were mistaken, we've confirmed she is Gillian Collins."

Emma started crying hysterically, Craig broke down, my dad cried out, "Why?"

I sat there stunned, staring at the floor, and said, "I'll believe it when I see it."

The policewoman said, "We will need someone to identify the body." She looked at my dad, who looked at me. She looked at Craig who looked away.

"I'll do it," I said.

I didn't volunteer because the men were wrestling with it, I volunteered because I knew myself well enough by then to know that if I didn't view her body I would go on looking for her to the end of my days, thinking they had it all wrong. Even many years later I dreamed, and sometimes daydreamed, that she would turn up suddenly and say: "Of course they had it wrong, Sam. I was in Australia having a secret life on the beach." In fact, it wouldn't surprise me if she called up today to say she had had an affair with President So-and-so, and she's sorry we missed her but she'd had a lovely time!

It would be much worse if I didn't identify her myself.

The policewoman took me into the viewing section of the morgue with a big glass window. It smelt weird and looked sterile. I was cold. I felt my legs buckle as I prepared for what was coming. For a moment I blanked and drifted off somewhere... I could hear the delighted shriek of a young child, "Swing me higher, Mum, higher!" I was in Queen Elizabeth Park with Mum and Emma. I was swinging so high and the sun shone down on us. A picnic was waiting. And I was completely happy.

Someone nudged me gently. Mum lay in front of me on a gurney covered in a white sheet on the other side of the window, all except for her head. I'd never seen a dead person before. Dead people are dead. Strange to say, I guess, but she looked unreal, as if made of plastic, like someone had created a mannequin of her. She didn't look peaceful or tortured or sad or happy. She didn't look like anything. She wasn't there.

I accepted her death right then and knew I needed to step up and get practical. Emma was not doing well. Dad was a mess. Craig looked devastated. Someone needed to grow up and sort this out, and it might as well be me. In that moment, every piece of the playful child inside me disappeared. I hardened and snapped to attention. I started organizing information, trying to figure it all out. The police gave me her bag. I searched it with the hope of piecing together a timeline. I wanted to understand exactly how she ended up in that hotel room, still convinced she was on her way to visit me.

I found a Burger King receipt time-stamped at around 5 p.m. the night before. She never was big on fast food. Then I remembered the chocolate cake. Was she indulging because she wouldn't have to diet anymore? Then I recalled her mention of the man who killed himself in the shed. Had she planned this so far back? Was she on her way to visit me and stopped at the hotel knowing if she met me she would lose her nerve or that I would talk her out of it? The police still hadn't located her blue Mini Cooper and she had paid for her hotel room in advance, all of which made me wonder if something sinister happened. Why would you pay for your hotel room in advance if you were going to kill yourself? My twenty-one-year-old self rationalized everything, but it was short-lived once I found the receipts for over the counter painkillers and a bottle of vodka, both found in her system.

And then the police told me about a note. I insisted they let me read it because, again, it would help make it a reality and give me closure. Mostly, the note was a classic fuck you. She matter-of-factly said she didn't want to live anymore; she didn't like her job, her daughters were away from home, she was unhappy all the time, and she still loved my dad even though she couldn't stand him. She said this would be best for everybody. It was no cry for attention or "I'll take an overdose if you don't hurry and get here" kind of suicide note. It was a decision. Even the hotel she chose stood across the street from where she'd met my dad in Piccadilly Circus—a fact not lost on him—and 50-miles away from where she lived, eliminating the chance any of us would find her body.

The letter didn't mention me at all, which bothered me. I justified this by reaffirming to myself that she knew me and how I would handle it, and that I would help Emma. She had said to me a few weeks before, "I won't leave until you're both gone from home." I didn't realize what she meant until I read the note. She meant she intended to leave the world, and she had been building up her courage for a long time, planning it all along.

People who die by suicide live in tremendous emotional pain and truly believe there is no other solution. They have no sense of the future, which is incredibly sad, because the future is what drives us and gives us passion and vision in life. To have no sense of future is to be hopeless. My mum was at that point. One of her favorite catchphrases was: "Stop this merry-go-round, I want to get off." We always thought she was only being funny, but in hindsight I can sense her pain.

It may seem strange but, in a way, I admire her for taking her own life this way. I think it takes guts and total determination to die by suicide. She was not a victim, she did it because she believed it was the best thing for her. I think she looks down now and says, "No, it was not a good idea," but at the time it felt right.

#

In many religions, especially Judaism, committing suicide is never the way to go. We were left unsure of what to do about her funeral and where to bury her. Emma was convinced our mum wanted to be buried next to her mother in a Jewish cemetery in Essex, outside London—a prestigious and expensive place where all that side of our family is buried.

I was a student with no money, Emma wasn't working, and my mum was in deep debt, much of which my Dad would have to pick up. The only valuable possession she owned was an antique diamond engagement ring belonging to her mother. Mum always told me I would have it one day and as much as I wished not to sell it, we didn't have any other options. I asked Emma for the ring. She told me Mum had pawned it when they were at their most desperate, which was omitted from the retelling of their Australian adventure. I was shocked. What's more, it meant we were left with only one option—talking to Uncle Harry.

My grandmother's brother, Uncle Harry, was instrumental in the family disowning my mum and disinheriting her as punishment for marrying my Catholic dad. Everyone in the family knew why she was on the outs, and I despised Harry for it; especially now, the morning after identifying my mum's body. But, Uncle Harry was also incredibly successful and very rich, with a lot of connections and, more than likely, he could help. I hated being so desperate, but I imagined once we explained the extreme situation, he would have compassion.

At first, we were welcomed inside the well-to-do home in St. John's Wood and seated in comfortable overstuffed leather chairs. Uncle Harry looked intimidating, rather like Anthony Hopkins playing it tough. His wife was beautiful and immaculately dressed, but aloof. She coolly offered us something to eat. I hadn't eaten since the student union in Liverpool over 24-hours earlier, so I accepted. They brought out bananas and a rich fruitcake. I took a banana and before I peeled it, started telling our predicament.

I didn't expect to be shown the door so quickly.

"It's ludicrous!" said Uncle Harry, flushed. "You're asking to bury a suicide in our family plot? For one thing, it goes against all tradition. It's ludicrous to suggest she be buried next to my sister, and outrageous to suggest I pay for it! Please leave."

Emma immediately burst into tears, and she and my dad stood up to walk out. I fumed, furiously indignant. Something deep inside me demanded I stay seated in that fancy armchair while something else deep inside me demanded I throw the banana at Uncle Harry. It bounced off his chest and fell to the floor with a dull thud. Uncle Harry stood with his mouth open like he wanted to say something, but was unable.

"What are you doing?" My dad said through his teeth, also astounded. "Get up, we're going."

"I'm not leaving," I said, looking Uncle Harry in the eye. "And I'm not going to eat anything until you arrange it so she is buried next to her mother." I surveyed the room, everyone's mouth was hanging wide open. "If your sister was alive right now, and could see how you're acting, she would be so appalled and so desperately upset that you are doing this horrible thing."

"Sam," said Dad, "let's go."

"I said I'm not leaving."

My eyes never left Uncle Harry. The room fell completely quiet, except for Emma's helpless sobs and my dad's intervention, which only served to make me more adamant. I wasn't moving and I would stay there until I starved. I was on a hunger strike.

"Right," Harry said, "excuse me." He left the room. We could hear him talking, was he on the phone? Was he actually calling the police? He appeared again after a few tense minutes, and looked at me.

"It's done," Uncle Harry said, "she has a place."

I wasn't happy. I wasn't sad. I felt mainly hatred. I hated Harry, I hated my dad, I hated the world and most of all, I hated myself for not seeing all this coming so I could do something to help my mum get through.

Harry had rightly judged that I wouldn't leave that seat—not after an hour, nor a week, nor a month. It amazes me to this day how in one breath it couldn't possibly happen for a thousand reasons, we have all these traditions about suicide, we have this long waiting list for the cemetery, we have no money to pay for this, it will never happen, it's outrageous; and yet, with one phone call from Uncle Harry, Mum got her spot next to her mother.

Sometimes when life seems the most insurmountable, or when someone tells you it can't be done, when challenged a little—even with only a banana—you can make them understand that it absolutely can be done.

#

Dark clouds blew a chilling wind that cut right through us. "It's bitter," Mum would have said. Because we were not brought up Jewish, the funeral service in Rainham, Essex felt unreal. We didn't understand a word of the service, entirely in Hebrew, which added to our despair. There were many people in the synagogue: other family, friends, and some I didn't recognize from her office. Mostly I kept my head straightened, my expression blank—never letting on to my family of hypocrites that I was on the verge of crumpling up and dying of heartache. Where were they when she needed them? I hated them all for not seeing this coming either.

At the conclusion of the service inside the chapel, the Rabbi made a small cut in my clothing as a symbol of the custom of tearing one's clothes in mourning. Despite it being bitterly cold and the rain falling, I wore the blue and white summer denim jacket Mum wore the day we said goodbye at the train station. Emma has the jacket to this day.

The skies grew darker and the rain drizzled away as we all walked slowly down to the gravesite. Mum's body was laid in a basic wooden coffin, which in Judaism symbolizes coming in with nothing and going out with nothing. A fair way to look at it I think.

Emma brought a little stereo, and at the end of the traditional part of the funeral as everyone left Emma and I began our own little service. She played Unchained Melody by the Righteous Brothers as we sat at the graveside. It was sad, but a little comedic at the same time. Everyone left Mum's graveside one by one, until only my sister and I were left, playing one of my mum's favorite songs on this little boom-box.

Oh my love, my darling

I've hungered for your touch

A long, lonely time

And time goes by so slowly

And time can do so much

Are you still mine?

I need your love

I need your love

God speed your love to me

As a pair of gravediggers filled the grave to the beat of the music, we knew she would have thought it was funny. There are no flowers in a Jewish cemetery, but the rows of white grave markers look a bit like a beach. Mum always loved the beach, a sun worshipper if ever there was one; always outside, smelling of coconut Ambre Solaire tanning lotion.

"Please look after our mum," Emma said to the gravediggers, choking up with a desperately tragic voice. They said they would. Emma also came up with the wording on the gravestone, which read: Gillian Collins — Our best friend fell asleep today. She was buried one plot over from her mother. We secured everything we could have wanted, for something we would never ever want.

I didn't suspect it at the time but I sank into a deep depression, which would hang over me for a very long time. My mind blurred in shock, disbelief, and an incredibly dark sadness. How could I possibly live even one day without my best friend, the person I loved most in the whole wide world? For the next decade I thought about Mum with sadness and confusion on the average of once every few minutes. When I'd hear people say of loved ones, "I think of them every day," I'd think how infrequent once a day seemed.

#

Ten years later, in 2002, I took a Tony Robbins personal development course in Australia. As an exercise we were required to write a letter of gratitude to someone who had done something upsetting in the course of our lives. So, on the 24-hour flight home from Brisbane back to London I wrote a letter to my mother.

Dear Mum, I am grateful for you committing suicide because...

Wow. Not an easy sentence to complete. But as I wrote down my gratitude list I realized if she had not died, it's likely I would have organized my life around our relationship. Attending university in Liverpool was about as far away from her as I ever wanted to go, and if she were alive and living in England today, odds are I would be nearby, never doing any of what I have done, avoiding many experiences that came my way, including starting Aspire. What happened to my mum ignited a passion and drive in me, which I needed for my business. Writing that letter made me realize my mum had given me a fantastic gift.

Many years later, Emma and I made a special visit to the gravesite on the twentieth anniversary of Mum's death. We called it a day of celebration. We missed Mum and celebrated how we had both made it, honoring the emotional gifts she gave to us. Yes, we have had our ups and downs over the years, but both of us rose up from those failures and went on to bigger and better lives. We were amazed at the lives we created, and especially at how normal we turned out.

My mum faced a tremendous failure when she couldn't make a go of it in Australia. She returned seeming broken and her ego deflated. At first I thought she had rebounded, and I dearly wish she could have learned the same lesson she taught her daughters, but it wasn't to be.

Immediately after Mum died, I settled three ideas in my mind. First, I vowed to learn as much as I could about psychology and having a strong mind so I wouldn't fall into the same traps as my mum. Second, I learned you can't trust anyone to tell you what is really going on inside their head, and you need to have your radar up to detect when people need help. Third, I decided that life is short and began trying to maximize all my experiences.

But as I grow older, I no longer believe that life is short. Today, I believe life is usually long with plenty of time to experience and enjoy it to the fullest. But you must be determined to control your experience, regardless of whatever or whoever is against you.

It's a sad fact that suicide rates among middle-aged Americans rose by nearly a third in the last decade, according to the Center for Disease Control. This is the largest increase among any age group and their research suggests the focus on suicide prevention should be shifted to adults aged 35 to 64. While the suicide rate among women rose faster than for men—31.5% to 27.3%, respectively—men are still more likely to die by suicide. The wider availability of prescription drugs may also contribute to the rise, as suicide by poisoning, including drug overdose, has risen 24.4% since 1999. We need to do more to support both women and men on the verge of suicide and the families they leave behind.

I want to also encourage you to find gratitude in the darkest moments of your life and be driven to be more successful as a result of what is going against you. Make a habit of asking yourself, 'What's the bigger message for me here?' When you think about the most challenging times in your life, focus on what you are grateful for and remember what it taught you. Make it empower you!

My mum taught me that. Thank you, Mum. As she used to say, "Don't let the bastards get you down!"

In Mum's case, they had succeeded in bringing her down. I learned over time, however, that everything happens for a reason and we need to find a positive meaning in even the most difficult experiences. Those are times that "make us or break us"—and that, too, is a conscious choice. So let your hardest times drive you to be a better person. Whatever is going on that you think you can't control, you always have control of yourself and of your own thoughts and feelings.

Sometimes you have to tune in to get back in control. Close your eyes, let go of judgmental thoughts and fears, breathe slowly, and ask yourself: what am I grateful for here? How do I choose to be? And what is it that is required of me as a result?

Even in the hardest moments, Radio Heaven has a message for us, but we have to tune in first, and then trust our feelings enough to act on them. Women are often told that we are "too emotional" or "too fluffy" when listening to our gut instincts. I believe that our intuition is the most important thing we have, and our homes and workplaces need more of it, not less. If a 21-year-old, brokenhearted student can cause a powerful and successful businessman to recognize his error and change his behavior with a banana, what can you accomplish?

CHAPTER 2

Council Estate Kid

"I wonder what's out there," I said to myself, looking out of my bedroom window over the flat rooftops of the council estate. Past the rooftops lay a gigantic grassy hill, beyond which I could not see. "Out... there," I sighed. Perhaps there was a big blue ocean, or maybe even California.

We had an uncle, Gerry, who lived in California, and Mum told me everyone there was always happy and the sun shone every day. We were saving money in a large jar on the window ledge in the living room so we could go and visit him someday. Except whenever the jar was nearly full, it mysteriously emptied again.

Today was another cold and drizzly English day.

I wish I lived in the sunshine! I thought.

Well, I'd speculated about that distant hill since the age of four. Now that I was five, I was done speculating, it was time to go find out what lay beyond the dreary council estate where we lived.

As Emma watched TISWAS (Today is Saturday, Wear a Smile) on the TV downstairs, I loaded up my school backpack with some candy and an apple juice and set off into the wild frontier. The walk was longer than I expected, taking nearly an entire chocolate bar to make it almost to the top, but I never looked back. I was headed to California to visit Uncle Gerry, feel the sunshine on my face and be where everyone was always happy.

And when I arrived at the top of the hill, do you know what I saw?

Nothing. It was an ordinary hill, flat at the top, with a few other houses and another big hill in the distance. And no chocolate left to propel me any further. Disappointed, I turned around to look at where I'd come from, and standing atop this great hill, which I'd conquered all by myself, I was flooded with a five-year-old version of awe. It could have been Mount Everest the way my heart pounded. It had taken at least twenty minutes to get up there, but when you're five, twenty minutes may as well be twenty hours. I lingered for a bit, getting accustomed to the newborn adventurer inside myself. I am a real-life explorer now! After a few moments, my tummy rumbled and I missed my mum. I started on the long trek back, unaware of the stir my adventure had caused back at base-camp.

As my dad drove up in our tiny red "Fanny" Fiat I felt only relief at knowing I would not to have to walk all the way home. I waved to him and saw through the windshield he was biting on his bottom lip, the tell tale sign he was upset about something.

"Where the bloody hell have you been?" he said, sticking his flushed face out of the window of the tiny car, as it screeched to halt. He had obviously driven all over the council estate, panicked, angrier than I had ever seen him before. He jumped out of the car and grabbed me. "Get in!" he said, shoving me inside.

All the way home, he fumed and bombarded me with questions intended to reveal what was the matter with me. I was honestly surprised my dad was so angry. What specifically about today would make him shove me into the car and swear at me? And even more surprising to me was that his anger was centered on me wandering off. I hadn't actually wandered off, I had planned an expedition, there was a difference but it was all lost on him. He didn't want to hear about my adventures. When we arrived home, my mum was crying hysterically.

All this awakened me to the fact that, as much as I loved my parents, we looked at life differently. I won't say that I haven't gained more perspective and appreciation for their caring attitude now. Many years later, I experienced the same intense fear and shock when my own four-year-old son, Jake, took it a step further, embarking on his own expedition out of pre-school alone, apples not falling far from trees, and all.

We had lived on a council estate (the English equivalent of a government housing project for those living on low income) for as long as I could remember. Before Emma was born, we lived in a small one-room flat in a questionable area of North West London. In 1972, when I was nine-months old, the government started to promote a scheme to help young families out of the inner city and into the suburban green counties around London. The well-meaning government intended for young couples to be able to rent a house for the first time and get closer to good jobs in suburban areas, an attempt to reduce the problems of a troubled city. However, well-intentioned and hard-working people, like my parents, weren't the only kinds of people invited to join the exodus. So, from a rough area of London, a rough area in the upscale home county of Hampshire was born.

We lived on the council estate because we struggled financially. I was conscious of this growing up, but never self-conscious. When all you know is a life with no frills, it's normal to make sure you are not a burden. I took our financial situation as seriously as I took every situation as a child—seriously enough that I once outgrew my shoes and didn't tell anyone.

I owned only one pair of shoes and they were getting tighter every day for a few weeks. I figured we couldn't afford new ones, and I did not want to add to the financial shortage, nor did I wish to upset my mum who always seemed stressed about money. I only wanted to help and I loved my mum, so not only did I not complain about my shoes, I was determined to wear them even if my toes start to bleed (that's what I told myself, anyway.)

The pain of my too-tight shoes grew unbearable and my schoolwork started to suffer, which was unacceptable in our family. My parents took notice and I was forced to tell my mother the reason. She burst into tears and hugged me like she would never let go. I didn't understand this at the time, but I knew she wasn't angry. And even though I was learning to be a frugal little girl, I was also relieved to learn we had enough for new shoes.

As a little girl, any money we had was earned by my dad who worked tirelessly at a local factory. My dad didn't know that my stay at home mum would often run up large credit card bills and not tell him. And I was heavily involved in the plot to keep him in the dark.

I awoke each morning earlier than everyone else, so my mum instructed me to snatch the mail up as it came through our letterbox and hide it until my dad left for work. I then dutifully delivered the credit card bills to my mum, always happy to help. Much of our life hovered around the subject of money, and I remember more than a few heated arguments between my mum and dad over it. Extra money would come, eventually, but not for a long time yet.

When I was seven and Emma five, my mother began complaining of severe lower back pain, lying on a hard floor for hours to make it better, but as soon as she would get up and start doing housework the healing was undone. Finally, she was diagnosed and hospitalized for a slipped disc, the treatment was six months in traction.

As miserable as Emma and I were when she was away, we sensed even more misery for our dad, who tried his best to keep our life together, working long hours to keep our financial ship afloat, taking care of two daughters, and now doing the cooking and cleaning Mum used to do.

There was no extra money for childcare, of course, but that problem was eased once he arranged for us to stay after school with Ruth, one of our neighbors.

Besides being incredibly kind, Ruth could sew fantastically. She made clothing, toys, and whatever else a little girl could possibly want. She was so thoughtful, and all our dolls were regularly kept in new outfits for as long as she watched over us. When I showed true interest in the magical box of scrap fabric and buttons underneath her sewing machine, she started teaching me to sew, opening a new world of creativity.

When time came to leave Ruth's house each day at 6 p.m., we would walk the short distance home, meet Dad, and pile into the car making it to the hospital in time for visiting hours. We chatted with Mum while she ate her dinner and then drove back home where Dad would make a pretty miserable dinner.

Heinz baked beans are a universal food in England. If you are on a budget, or you want to eat something quick and filling, it's a tin of baked beans on toast. Except we didn't have fresh bread while mum was in hospital. So every night Dad took a can of baked beans and a can of spaghetti in tomato sauce and poured them both into the same bowl. A few minutes in the microwave, an unceremonious "ding," and dinner was served. The same dinner was served, in fact, almost every night for six months (aside from the rare takeaway from the fish and chip shop on the way home from the hospital).

We never once complained. Our mum lay in the hospital in complete misery, we were broke, and Dad was doing his best. If that's what we could afford to eat, it was my job to accept it and make sure Emma acted okay with it too.

After dinner was finished, I washed the dishes. We didn't have a dishwasher, so everything awaited me in the kitchen sink. I wasn't tall enough to reach, so I stood on a kitchen stool, rolled up my sleeves and dug in, but there was more than dishes in the sink. My dad was a smoker back then and threw spent matches and stinky cigarette butts in the sink, along with the sharp-edged empty cans of beans and spaghetti. This created a foul smelling grey stew, but since I was responsible for the dishes each night, I cleaned to the best of my ability.

What I didn't know, and my dad didn't realize, was that handling cigarette butts and tin cans and submerging your hands in dirty water would cause an infection under my fingernails, which turned green like little lily pads. There wasn't much pain and my mum or dad or teachers never questioned it, so I didn't mention it to avoid causing any extra stress.

One day while we visited Mum at the hospital, an attending nurse came in to check on her and happened to notice my hands. "What happened to your fingers?" she asked. But it was the way she asked the question that tipped me off. I sensed immediately that if I told the truth someone was going to be in trouble—could be me, could be my parents— but as of now, all eyes were on me.

"What do you mean?" I said, looking at my fingers like I had never seen them before, attempting to be as vague as possible.

The nurse didn't need me to tell her what was wrong, she wanted to get to the bottom of it. She took my wrists and moved in for closer inspection. "You have poisonous fingers!" she said.

Outside I kept my cool, but inside I filled with dread. Poisonous fingers! I looked down as my dad's face signaled the coming thunder. Poisonous fingers and Dad—I need to get out of here!

"You need to be treated right away, wait here," said the nurse. She grabbed me by the hand and marched me down the hall for treatment.

I was delighted to get rid of my poisonous fingers. But, even better, I didn't have to do dishes anymore. From then on, my dad did the dishes each night, and my fingers healed fine.

I have learned that most of the time, people in difficult circumstances try to do the best they can. Sometimes it's a matter of making it through

the rough patch and hanging on to what they already have. Oth
if it's not working right or they have stalled, they will get a v
an angel who gives them a push in a new direction or averts wnaτ ιs
happening altogether. That day, my angel was the nurse. Before that,
Ruth was my angel. There would be more visits to come.

We often experience inexplicable emotions when faced with a difficult
environment, disappointment, or other hard choices. Sometimes we can
get so attached to the "poor me" in the story that we turn into unhappy
victims, unaware of our opportunities, and easily taken advantage of by
toxic people who are perfectly happy to sit and complain with us, egging
us on.

Plenty of circumstances were against me as a kid: my mum was in the
hospital, we were always broke, and I had poisonous fingers. I certainly
could have let this train of thinking run my life as easily as others I knew
had allowed it to run theirs. But I observed early on it didn't do them any
good, and it only depressed them further.

I've since learned two fundamentals, which shape what we are: our
personality as children and the environment we grow up in. It is both
nature and nurture. I was born independent, born to exploration and
creativity. I find these strengths come easily and are fun for me. I've also
learned through experience how to handle money well, witnessing its
mismanagement firsthand. As an adult, I love to save money, I never use
credit cards and have little debt.

I am always at my happiest and most successful when I play to the
same childhood strengths I still have today as an adult. Being authentic
to your original nature, and the nurture you had in the environment you
grew up in, will do the same for you. What is needed is to maintain hope
and remain true to yourself, remembering your nature and strengths as a
child, and the positive outcome of your unique upbringing and journey,
which formed who you are.

Some might say, "All well and good, but what happens if you face something in your environment that you can't overcome on your own?"

When that point arrives, support often comes—sometimes it's a teacher, or a nurse, or an insight from Radio Heaven to give us hope. My supporters were always coming to the rescue when I needed them, and yours will too. You can probably remember a few of them right now, if you concentrate. So be continuously alert to who your advocates are, no matter how small the issue, and think about what you can learn from them. Remember, sometimes they come from the least expected places.

It is also important to review your environment, as even a negative one can shape you positively and energize your future. It is easy to blame circumstances for the life choices we make. When we unconsciously let the people around us turn us into victims, we end up leading lives of complaint, blame, and hopelessness. Instead, let these people and situations drive you to get out to explore the best possible you.

CHAPTER 3

Bully Trouble

"Dad," I said, my bottom lip quivering slightly.

"Yes, Sam, what is it?" He said not looking up from the broken radio he was fixing.

"Dad, I don't want to go outside."

"Why?" He looked up briefly, then back down when I hesitated.

"Aileen Mersh is sitting in the square and she's going to get me." I started to cry.

After a few moments he finally looked up at me and said, "Well, you're going to have to stand up for yourself someday, might as well start now. Go on, get outside."

"But I don't want to go outside. I can't," I repeated.

Dad glared at me, frustrated by the disturbance to his amateur radio hobby. He took hold of my hand and walked me to the front door, opened it, pushed me outside, and closed the door behind me.

According to the American Academy of Child and Adolescent Psychiatry, nearly half of all school children are bullied sometime during primary or secondary school, and a minimum of ten percent are bullied regularly. Child bullying is a serious problem around the world and in some serious cases, depression and suicide attempts can result from being bullied.

Standing up to bullies, whether for yourself or for the rights of others, is fundamental. Sometime it is necessary to fight for the rights of our children, a friend, a team, an organization or a community. The world needs people to put their head above the parapet and say: "You are not allowed to do this."

Bullies were a big problem for me, and they terrorized my childhood. Even though being at home was safe, I would often spy bullying kids or gangs outside our house on the council estate. Since I didn't know they couldn't see in through our lace net curtains, I would run past the windows in the living room to avoid detection; I figured if they didn't know I was at home, they wouldn't lie in wait for me to come out.

I did this for seven years.

Our council estate consisted of grids of flat roofed housing around a small square of grass with a tree and bench and a haphazard grouping of trees at one end. We lived on one side of the square, the Mersh family lived in the house directly across from us. I use the term family loosely, as it is unlikely the men who rotated through that house every few weeks were all named Mersh. The oldest daughter, Aileen, was the same age as me, and we could have played together if not for the fact that she wanted me dead for no apparent reason.

To be fair, most of the bullying from other kids was kid-stuff, I could handle it. I learned to keep my head up, swear, swagger, and fiercely protect Emma. But Aileen's bullying was different, somehow darker, more volatile, and much more random. Where other bullies seemed mostly to be relieving boredom at the expense of smaller children, Aileen played for keeps—she intended to hurt you.

In my dad's efforts to help me stand up for myself, he and I attended a martial arts class, which I endured for a few years to appease him. All those Karate moves would have worked fine if my opponents stood still for me—or were napping, perhaps.

Determining my parents were not going to help much, I took matters into my own hands. I never mentioned bullying, my fears, or anything else unpleasant, letting them think everything was fine. Rather, I opted for more strategic movements whenever leaving the house or playing around the neighborhood. I would meticulously plan trips outside, playing on the other side of the estate where no one else congregated, riding my bike with Emma away from the area where my bullies lay in wait, or playing near the shops. I only left the house when I was sure no one was watching, and I would get back as secretly and stealthily as possible. I learned both to live in fear and successfully hide it from my parents.

By twelve years old my hair had grown halfway down my back. My dad loved my hair and I often received compliments from other people, but my relationship with my hair was love/hate. I loved the compliments, certainly, but having such luxurious locks in my neighborhood made me an easy target, especially for Aileen. I always came off worse in a fight with her because she would grab hold of my hair, an easy takedown which hurt all the way to the floor.

I was over my hair, concluding that it was strategically impractical and dangerous. One day Mum dropped me off at the hairdresser for a trim while she continued on to shop. The hairdresser did exactly as instructed—by me! At last I had an extremely short, bowl-style haircut; unflattering but effective. I can still remember my mum's gasp outside the hairdresser, and my dad's shock and anger when we walked through the door.

To me it was simple logic, so I explained the problem and solution to him one more time. He huffed and walked off. What could he do about it now, glue it back on? Besides, he never would have allowed it even if I had asked permission. My short hair worked great, of course, and gave me renewed confidence. Aileen had nothing to get hold of now.

I quickly discovered the power of making my own decisions and taking control even if my parents didn't love the idea. I've also kept my hair short most of my life and I love how confident it still makes me feel.

But for all those long years on the council estate, I only ever wanted one thing: to get away from Aileen Mersh. You see, she wasn't only my neighbor, she also attended my junior school, forcing me to deal with her on a daily basis.

When time came for senior school, I was overjoyed to discover that it was possible to go to a different school and escape Aileen. It was farther away, but I could not care less as long as Aileen couldn't harass me anymore—the further away, the better. I fantasized about how great life would be without her sitting on the bench in front of my house every day, waiting for me to come outside so she could torture me.

I found the courage to run this notion past my parents. I presented the case with an attorney's precision, and even though my desire to get away from Aileen bordered on obsession, I acted perfectly cool and rational during my presentation. It was a better school (true), I had some friends there (not true, but so what) and I was more than willing to walk the extra distance in the interest of better education (sort of true).

Their only objection was the longer walk.

"No problem," I said, "I thought of that, of course, and I don't mind walking further. In fact, it's only ten minutes more. It will be good exercise and it's a better school, after all." I rested my case.

When they agreed there wasn't a happier girl in the council estate. This was a life changing moment for me, discovering I could alter the course of history by sheer force of will. With Aileen out of the picture, with new confidence and excitement, I could handle whatever life had in store for me next.

What life had in store for me next was Aileen's expelling from her school and being sent to mine. I couldn't believe it. I immediately resumed looking over my shoulder and then up ahead as far as I could to check the routes for any sign of Aileen. If the coast was clear, I would run all the way to the bridge to get close to other kids on the way to school. If I could get that far, the likelihood of her picking me to bully diminished significantly with all the other fresh meat around.

One day I noticed she wasn't there. I lingered a few extra moments to make sure. Maybe she was home with the flu? Maybe she was in hospital with a severe case of cold sores? Who cared, the coast was clear! Enjoying a rare treat, I skipped alongside the brook.

Huge mistake.

There she sat, hiding behind some overgrown bushes, lying in wait where her unsuspecting victims couldn't spot her. Her game had improved.

"Sam Collins," she called. "Come here."

I was trapped. A fenced field at the junior school lay on my right, the impassable brook sloshed quietly on my left; there was no other place to run where she couldn't nab me. Dread flooded all through me and my hands shook. I resigned to my fate as she approached, a smug look on her face. She knew she had me.

"Guess what?" she said, poking me in the face with her finger. "You're not going to school today."

I was crying inside, but I was determined to not cry in front of her. She was too close to me to make a run for it, but I took a desperate look behind me anyway. I didn't expect to see another girl wearing our school uniform walking up behind us. I'd never seen her before.

It should have felt relieved, but when I locked eyes with the unknown girl I could tell she was equally nervous. Aileen's notoriety preceded her, and whether she picked on you or not, you went out of your way to avoid her trouble. I fully expected this girl to keep walking, and honestly I wouldn't have held it against her if she had, but inside me there glimmered some desperate hope. The mystery girl didn't walk by, she walked deliberately toward us and then stood directly between Aileen and me.

She looked straight at Aileen and said, "You're not allowed to do this."

"Fuck off, nigger!" Aileen snarled, her expression instantly changing from hostility to something nearer confusion at being directly confronted. I was shocked she had said the F-word, but I didn't know what the other word meant.

"Who do you think you are?" said Aileen.

I turned to the new girl in one of those surreal, slow motion movie moments. Aileen could have started juggling flaming coconuts and singing Bingo Was His Name-o and I wouldn't have noticed.

"Who am I?" the mystery girl said, "I'm your worst enemy if you don't leave us alone."

There were a few moments of Mexican stand-off style silence. Aileen actually took a step back. Seizing the moment, my brand new best friend took my shaking hand and marched with me up the brook path to school, our heads held high, victorious. No other kid, not even a boy, had stood up to Aileen before, let alone left her speechless.

"Don't look back", she said.

From that day on I spent every possible moment with Marsha Gordon.

My new best friend, Marsha, was the only black girl in the entire neighborhood. She had big braces on her teeth and big glasses, no glamour puss. (Not yet, anyway. When we grew up she looked like the singer Sade. Gorgeous.) But she was gorgeous in all the inside ways that truly count. She was a caring person who stood up for the rights of others. And she was pretty much my only friend at the time.

We were an odd pair at school. I was studious and quiet while Marsha was theatrical and outgoing. But because she was black, she was even more an outcast than me. If it bothered her, I couldn't tell, because she knew herself and more importantly, truly liked herself. Well, I liked her, too. The color of her skin never even registered with me, and being her friend was one of the greatest life experiences I had ever had. Being her friend was all that mattered to me.

As for Aileen, she didn't bother us much more after that day. I was too young then to understand why Aileen wanted to hurt people. I would later learn that bullies often have a lot of issues at home. I would also come to learn that bullies are not always who we suspect: sometimes they are other children, sometimes parents, sometimes they are our bosses or board members and they can be male or female. Sometimes we are uncomfortably looking at our bully in the mirror. Are you ever a bully? Even unconsciously?

Even though there were other childhood friends before and after Marsha Gordon, she is the one I remember best. She taught me so much about the power of friendship simply through being my friend. She taught me the importance of standing your ground, simply by standing hers. She didn't walk by when she came across someone in trouble. She taught me not to put my head down and put up with a bully who was so embedded in my daily routine it seemed normal. She helped me be more confident about defending against what was not allowed. She also helped me face one of my worst fears, even though I was a stranger to her at the time. Her influence directly helped me later on with Uncle Harry, and today with many of the dominant senior men I encounter on a daily basis through Aspire.

It is fundamental to stand up to bullies and we cannot do it alone. It is empowering to stand up for what's right; to stand up for others, for a cause that is close and personal. Find your allies and stand up together. Bullies are troubled cowards at heart, and some of the worst bullies are women, a saddening fact. There will always be people aiming to intimidate you, but what matters most is how you respond to it and the support you get to help you through it.

What or who is it time for you to stand up for?

CHAPTER 4

The Iron Lady

It was 1985: England re-elected Margaret Thatcher as Prime Minister, the economy was improving, and women were coming into the workforce in droves. After my mum's recovery from her back operations, and after 14-years of looking after me and Emma, she decided to return to work.

Mum's confidence exploded. But what I remember most about my mum heading off to work were her shoulder pads. Back then, huge shoulder pads were in fashion, sewn under the jacket and sometimes even the blouse. She wore a different power suit practically every day. My favorite was her red suit with giant black lapels and what I believed were the biggest shoulder pads in England at the time. The suit complimented her long black hair, immaculate make-up, and big costume jewelry.

The dramatic change in her whole being was obvious, even to fourteen-year-old me. She was my role model first as a wonderful mother who stayed at home and made life fun for her daughters, and second as a businesswoman who went happily off to work each day to help provide a better life for her family. Completely impressed, I determined then to get a job as soon as possible. I wanted so much to be like her; to work hard, make my own money, and find out what incredible felt like.

My job search began at the local Queensmead shopping center. I walked around to every shop (nearly fifty) asking if they offered any Saturday jobs. The ones who didn't say no, asked how old I was. When they found out, the answer was always the same: "Sorry, we don't take Saturday-girls until sixteen." Usually adding, "It's not long to wait, dear."

I trudged the two miles home down Beta Drive, the long road leading to our house, totally despondent. That evening at dinner, when I flopped into my chair, Mum knew something was up.

"What's wrong, Sam?" she said.

"I can't get a shop job because I'm fourteen and you have to be sixteen," I huffed. "It's not fair."

"Well, if you can't get a shop job, what else could you do? Why don't you think about it for a while and see what you can come up with?" My mum the businesswoman refused to allow me to feel sorry for myself. "I know you'll think of something."

After dinner, I sulked back to my room and sat on my bed. What other way could I make some money? After all, not everyone who works, works in a shop. My dad once told me how lots of people work for themselves, doing jobs for other people who have more money than time. The thought mesmerized me.

A while later, I came out of my room and asked my mum, "What's something that you don't like doing that I could do for you to earn some money?"

She thought about it for a moment. "Ironing," she said flatly. "I hate doing ironing - particularly my work suits. I really don't have the time anymore, either. If you do them for me properly, I'll pay you for each one you iron."

"How much?" I asked, beaming.

If you've never ironed a woman's power-suit from the 1980's before, let me tell you it isn't easy, especially around the collars and shoulder pads. I kept at it, even though my mum returned a few for a second ironing. But within a few weeks I was a pro. I made a bit of money, but even better, I knew exactly where my mum had gained her newfound confidence.

That's when my next idea came to me: If Mum doesn't like ironing, I wonder how many other women in the neighborhood don't like ironing? The next day, I put a little sign up in our local newsagent in the shop window, advertising ironing for hire at £3 (around $5) a basket. I drew some flowers around the edge of the card and gave our family home phone number in a bright yellow pen so you could really see it. I didn't tell my mum or dad about the advertisement since I wasn't sure about the response. Plus, my dad wouldn't like strangers calling the house. That night, three people rang! I dove for the phone twice, my dad picked up the last, telling them "Wrong number!" Still, I was in the ironing business now. My mum was on board immediately and took me to the houses to make sure everything was kosher, then she would drop me off and pick me up when I finished.

Great ideas often work this way. When we are new at something, such as ironing power-suits, it can be challenging. But as we practice and become more competent, it turns into confidence. Then humming along one day with seemingly nothing on our minds we'll tune into Radio Heaven—and a great idea appears as if out of thin air. When we concentrate exclusively on getting competent, rather than struggling to come up some big idea to solve all our problems, we make faster progress, put less performance pressure on ourselves, and have far less stress about the future as a result.

I did most of my ironing on Sunday mornings. Four neighbors paid me £3 per basket. A fourteen-year old girl making £12 a week in 1985 was nothing to sneeze at. I had flexible hours and worked only when

I wanted, and I hung out with great women like my mum who used to give me Coke to drink, let me watch TV and eat chocolate, and then left me alone to work. And the best part; I didn't have to wait two whole years to become a businesswoman like my mum.

Working for myself turned out to be a powerful lesson. I didn't need anybody's permission to work or make extra money, even as young as I was. I needed only to believe nothing stood in the way of my dream. With my mum's help and some questioning of the status quo, I ended up with a far better situation than I originally thought possible.

It was a powerful lesson in perseverance, too. I could have stopped my job search in its tracks, when people older than me or in a position of power said I couldn't work until sixteen. I didn't let it stop me, though. I didn't sit back and wait. Thus began my belief in entrepreneurialism.

When I did turn sixteen, I tried to be normal and found a job in a shoe shop in Queensmead shopping center. On my first Saturday, I sold more shoes with bags and belt accessories than the full-time staff from the week before and won their monthly employee incentive competition, except the female manager wouldn't give me the £25 voucher prize because I only worked Saturdays. I quit the next week deciding not to work for other people again. Why would I work more hours, for less pay and be stuck in a shop all day long being told what to do?

Turns out I wasn't alone in cottoning on to this idea—the number of businesses owned by women has increased 59% since 1997, according to an estimate from American Express. Those 8.6 million women-owned businesses generate more than $1.3 trillion in revenue and employ nearly 7.8 million people.

I was glad to learn about the power of owning my own business from an early age. Working for yourself is a great way to earn more money, have flexible hours and be responsible for your own destiny. Don't accept no, or be unwilling to rock the status quo. We should never let business as usual stand in the way of our dreams. Many of us do get stuck thinking that because someone in authority said no or here's how it is in an organization, society, or out in the world that we must automatically comply. We need to recognize this game—that it is, in fact, a game—and then stop playing. Right now I'm guessing you have recently been told 'no' to something or other. What is it you were trying to achieve? And what could you do to achieve the same outcome in a different way?

Developing a rule-breaking entrepreneurial approach is perfectly possible even if someone else employs you. When someone in authority tells you no, or you can't do something or your society has a status quo, make it your first instinct to look for a creative way around obstacles in front of you, not to simply fold and give up. You may be led to new ideas and the achievement of dreams you never thought possible.

CHAPTER 5

Anything A Boy Can Do

No one called me Samantha growing up, not even when I got into trouble. I was named after my mum's dad and grandfather, both named Samuel and both powerful men. My dad had no qualms about wanting a son, once telling me that every man wants a son and, "Had you been a boy, I would want success for you; as you are a girl, I still want success for you." I'm glad he took pains to be an equal-opportunities dad.

"You can do anything a boy can do," he would often say. "And since we're thumping above poor, there's only two ways out of this situation: crime or education. And I don't want you to be a crime boss."

When all the girls at school were enrolling in home economics, basically a cooking class, my dad encouraged me to take the metalwork class. I didn't particularly care to learn metalwork, but I figured there was no harm in trying, and my had already taught me all the cooking skills I would ever need, therefore, I'd have the best of both worlds.

Not surprisingly, I was the only girl in the class. And there were no shortage of comments from other girls questioning my choice, or confused looks from the boys at my presence in their workshop. I didn't mind the teasing (I had endured worse) and I enjoyed the idea of doing something other girls didn't have the courage to try. The boys were actually easier to deal with and once I demonstrated I was equally good at metalwork they left me alone.

My dad helped form my early views on equal opportunities and shaped my understanding about where women stand in terms of equal treatment in the world. Back in 1986, women had made great strides in the workforce, but it was still a different world compared to today. I have only recently begun to realize that my dad anticipated the change. He understood my potential and tried to give me the fundamentals to compete and, for that, I am extremely grateful.

When the time came to go to sixth-form college (that is, community college) my dad encouraged me toward math and sciences, and physics particularly. He believed Information Technology was the right career choice and would become a prized career in the near future (and he was certainly right about that). He talked about having a profession, job security, and being paid well; he now worked for IBM and possessed all of those, though he was often unhappy about being regularly passed over for promotion, due to his counter-cultural ways. I couldn't understand what was so great about a profession where you spent most of the week away from your family.

And I had no interest in IT or engineering. If you had presented me with a list of career alternatives and Computer Engineer was the only one offering the huge bonus, I'd still choose something else, but since he was right about the metalwork class, I gave him the benefit of the doubt and tried engineering. Maybe he knew me better than I thought?

I registered to take A-Level physics, math, and since I couldn't fully commit to pure science, one geography class. There was something about geography I couldn't resist. I always fancied myself as an explorer. I wanted nothing more than to get out of town, travel, and explore the seven seas. I still wanted to know what was out there, even if I couldn't go right then. I figured a geography class would at least show me where everything was.

Yet, I should have known engineering wasn't right for me from the way I absolutely lit up thinking about geography. It's times like these when it's most helpful to know yourself! All the proof I needed came loud and clear on the first day of class, as soon as I walked into the physics classroom. Sure enough, I was the only girl in the room again— no problem there, of course—but I really hated the class. If I wanted to change tracks, I had to get out of it right away before registration closed for the semester, which meant facing another long talk with my dad.

My dad hadn't completed his high school education, but he had high hopes for me, and let me know in no uncertain terms when I came home from junior school with a C-. The talking to was intense enough to remember even now. To my dad, only first place counted. This was also reinforced the time I returned home proudly showing off a third-place certificate I'd won at school and he ripped it in half in my face.

My father intended me to be the first of his family to go to university, the culmination of his personal dream. I was also to be first to pursue computing science. But no matter what I did, I was to be first overall. Since the junior school report incident, I had always earned good grades and tried my best so he would be kept happy and I'd be kept out of hot water. But I was also keen to learn about some subjects he considered complete garbage, or a waste of time and money.

So with no other choice, I drew up my courage and told him I didn't want to do physics or IT.

"Okay, Sam," he said through gritted teeth and a bit lip, "what do you want to do?"

"I want to do business studies."

"What sort of bloody subject is business studies?" he said. "You're absolutely not going to do business studies."

"Listen for a minute, Dad. I want to run my own business someday."

"People who run their own business don't need a degree to run their own business. They run their own business. Business studies is a subject for people who don't know what they want to do. Waste of time. Why go to school at all?"

"Please, Dad. I really want to do business studies."

"No," he said. "What else is there?"

I thought for a moment, trying to come up with another way to learn more about business.

"Well, what about economics?" I said. "I'll also keep mathematics and take the statistics option."

He thought for a moment, looked at me and said, "Okay." A resigned okay, but an okay nonetheless.

With the compromise struck, I studied economics, pure mathematics with statistics, and of course geography. I didn't love economics (and it certainly wasn't easy), but I loved geography like I thought I would. And, believe it or not, I even enjoyed statistics and absolutely loved pure mathematics. For one, math didn't involve doing any essays, meaning I didn't have to do research or a lot of writing, but I also enjoyed being able to exercise my logic and rational abilities.

Schoolwork was fine, but there were other extra-curricular activities going on at the college that I disliked more than engineering or taking hard classes. The school was in an affluent area of Hampshire and most of the kids were from well-off families—nothing wrong with that—but there were enough BMWs, Porsches and sports cars to start a luxury auto dealership in the parking lot, and those cars didn't belong to the instructors. The students appeared less interested in learning than they did in what you looked like, dressed like, and what family you were from, and especially, the amount of money your family earned.

I was seventeen, overweight, and raised on a council estate. As far as money went, well, we were doing okay now, but ours didn't go nearly as far as theirs. The school was not a fit for me and more than a few of my affluent peers openly reinforced that fact. Eventually, it was a real effort to get out of bed to go endure their juvenile oppression. How bizarre that these kids, who had nearly everything, could complain about anything in their lives, or their parents, or the teachers, or me. I put my head down and worked hard. It wasn't terrible, and I was physically safe, but I withdrew from most activities and felt far more comfortable studying than socializing.

Not to say I had no social life at all, because I met Andrew, my first boyfriend, at the store where he worked weekends on the deli counter. He was lovely, and we were a close couple. Everyone in both our families fully expected we would attend Portsmouth College together. Portsmouth was down the coast, a 40-minute drive from home. It was fine for a university, and I applied to up appearances and make everyone happy. I was accepted, but I had other plans for my life, if you hadn't already guessed.

In England, especially back then, this "north vs. south" way of thinking had taken root. If you lived in the south you stayed in the south and vice-versa. To southerners like us, anywhere north of Watford was full of coalmines and those northern people. But I was fascinated by the north, and frankly, couldn't wait to go and meet some of those rugged northern men I had heard so much about. And it was far away from stuck-up Farnborough, where I was at the time.

While I told everyone, including my parents and Andrew, that I would be going to Portsmouth, I had secretly applied to Liverpool, Manchester, and Leeds. All three schools were in the north, and all close to 300-miles from home. Even though England is a relatively small country, those 300-miles might as well be 3,000. Northern England was equally alien to southerners as the U.S., Canada, or South America. I wanted to explore, and those schools were about as far away as I could justify at the time; after all, I didn't want to be too far away from my mum.

Manchester was my first choice, and I dreamed up the men I'd meet in Manchester. I would find one to travel the world with me and we would end up living in sunny California by the beach with our lovely children. The dream was a good enough start.

One sunny Sunday, my parents and I with Andrew in tow, took a day-trip to Portsmouth to check out the University campus. They loved it, but I hated it. It all looked exactly the same as back home in Farnborough. I sensed it in my gut before we even pulled into the car park, it wasn't the university for me. As we toured the campus I kept mostly quiet. My dad gushed the entire time, "This is great! And it's by the sea! How lovely... Sam, isn't it lovely? Andy, what do you think?"

Boring!

As soon as I could get a moment, I pulled my mum aside and told her I had also applied to some other universities and was already accepted to Liverpool (not my first choice, but nearing the end of our Portsmouth tour, Liverpool sounded like heaven). Mum wasn't shocked. In fact, she was great about the news, as always, even acting as the diplomat later with my dad. She seemed to understand why I needed to get away from Farnborough and wisely knew I was old enough to make the decision myself.

"When we get back home you can take a train to Liverpool," she said. "You go on your own so we don't bias your view. Go up there and see how it feels."

That's exactly what I did. I was eighteen and on my first big exploration up north. I brought the necessities on the train with me, of course, my CD-player and new fave band "Everything But The Girl" on constant repeat. As the green fields of England whisked by me, my dreams seemed like they were already coming true. Just like on the car ride to Portsmouth, I made my decision before I had even arrived in Liverpool. Nothing could keep me from that big city filled with so many unique and wonderful personalities, and the birthplace of The Beatles.

Who wouldn't want to soak all of that in?

I loved Liverpool University as soon as I walked on the grounds. It was different, aggressive, and a bit edgy. I had a great visit, and when I came home to tell my mum, dad, and Andrew that I had made up my mind to go there instead, I was pleasantly surprised by how supportive they were.

"You need to do what you need to do, Sam," my dad said, "and we support you."

Who is this man?

Even Andrew opted not to go to Portsmouth. He attended Leeds instead so we could still see each other regularly. I'm not sure if my decision inspired him a little, but I'd like to think so. Unfortunately, our relationship didn't survive the long-distance and we agreed to break it off, which was okay because I was completely smitten with northern men.

The most important concept here is that we all have the ability to steer ourselves on the path for the future. When we set a bigger goal for ourselves, such as getting out of a hometown rut, and we follow through, the people in our life will usually start to support our vision. I think sometimes we stop ourselves from doing what we want because we care about what other people think—or invent what they might be thinking—more than we do about making a decision that might cause us to be isolated for a while. We defeat ourselves saying "So-and-so is going to hate this... they're going to be against me... maybe even sabotage me... this will never work out." Most of the time none of that is true. We sabotage ourselves before a word is ever spoken to anyone else.

Other people are generally supportive. Meaning whatever it is, they want the best for you because they love you. You don't need to worry over what people who don't love you think. Indeed, those people closest to us want us to be successful, even if they are scared for us, or it's something they wouldn't consider doing themselves, or their tolerance for risk is different. The tricky part is not letting their fears hold sway over our decisions. You must follow your heart, lest someone else's fear becomes your regret.

My parents drove me up to Liverpool for the start of my first year. Mum cried a lot and lamented how far away I would be. I would miss her, too. We were growing even closer as I reached the end of my teenage years. I wondered if I could actually be away from her for so long and promised myself to come home as many weekends and holidays as possible.

My new temporary home was another council estate, or a former one, anyway. It was a condemned tower block in Everton called Cander Towers, which the school had bought from the local council as temporary student dorms. Renovations were barely underway and construction still incomplete on the new campus, which included brand new student housing near the Anglican Cathedral in the center of town. Needless to say, this former council estate sat in one of the worst parts of the city and was twenty minutes by bus from the main campus.

Everton, a suburb of Liverpool, was easily in the top five worst places in the world to be a stranger at the time, but meant the skills I had picked up on my own council estate would come in handy, and the additional skills I would gain in Everton would serve me when I visited Democratic Republic of Congo in 2013. The main trick was to keep your head up, keep your mouth shut, and act like you had lived there all your life. Everton was the type of place where shops and gas stations had bulletproof glass and metal drawers for taking money and giving change. A place where you had to watch out for yourself.

Mum wasn't at all happy about delivering me to Everton.

I loved everything about Liverpool. I loved even the idea of being in Liverpool. But to be honest, my feelings about safety were mixed, too, now that we were actually standing out front of the student flats of Cander Towers, which I had not seen on my tour of campus. We walked in to see a wall full of graffiti, trash on the floors, and the smell of urine topping it all off. The elevator only sort of worked—it moved up and down but made highly questionable noises in the process. We considered it safer to walk up the seventeen floors to my dorm rather than risk getting stuck.

Despite the daunting entry, once we arrived at the flat I was immediately smitten by my flatmates. There was another Samantha from Chester, who had wild hair like a rock star, and was also called "Sam," and then there was Simone, so excited to meet me because she was also from the South. She looked like a petite beatnik with jet black, bobbed hair and wore cool hippie clothes. I instantly imagined the fun times ahead of the three of us, and I wasn't wrong.

My dad walked around, hands in his pockets like the place carried some kind of contagious disease. My mum, of course, sobbed her eyes out, bordering on hysterical about leaving me in the hands of a rock and roller and a hippie who she had only just met, not to mention the run-down building, unfit even to remain a council estate. Suddenly, though, I didn't want to hear it, and I wasn't afraid of Everton, or the elevator, or the old building. All I wanted to do was politely, but definitely, escort them out the door so I could get this new adventure underway.

"I'm fine," I kept telling them, "you two go ahead, it's a long drive home. Don't worry, I will be fine. I love you! I'll call you every day! I love you!"

Within seconds of the door-latch click behind them, a gut-wrenching pang took me by surprise. I was homesick. What a wimp!

My flatmates were wonderful, launching into action and dragging me to the student union for drinks. I sat in the back of the bus to the campus, sad enough to question my decision. I confessed to Sam and Simone, "My God, at home it seemed like such a good idea to be 300-miles away, and live in a completely different city, and now I'm not so sure." They were understanding about everything and tried their best to cheer me up but, while I had a good time with them, I felt foreign. I struggled with the prospect of spending the next four years in this far-off city, all alone. But I wasn't alone, not really. At least it wasn't Farnborough; and soon enough this wonderful city would be as familiar to me as my own hometown.

After drinks, we hailed two taxis. Why two? Because the first taxi to stop refused to take us to Everton! Eventually, we found another and as we rounded the corner approaching the Towers, our driver slowed the cab to a crawl, looking nervously around the street blocked by an ambulance, several police cars, and a throng of drunken students.

"Wow!" I said, looking up the length of the building, anticipating some exciting end to the first day of my new cosmopolitan life, "I wonder what's happening?"

We climbed out of the taxi and edged our way toward the front of Cander Towers, but nobody was allowed in. When we found out why, we did not find it exciting at all.

A girl had returned from having drinks at the student union, like us. They'd all gone up in the elevator, like we were about to, and the elevator got stuck. The girl climbed out to go for help, but once inside the elevator shaft she must have tripped. She fell sixteen-floors to her death.

It was her first night in Liverpool, just like me. The fact hit me like a ton of bricks. I never before entertained the idea that life was unpredictable, since mine was so sheltered up to then. It clarified the importance of living for what I loved right now, because waiting for tomorrow could be too late.

My first night in Liverpool, I fell asleep in a strange bed with my mind made up about two things: first, I would never take the elevator; second, I would always do what I felt in my gut was right for me. I would live my life to the fullest. I would take on this adventure, and any that lay ahead, with determination and enthusiasm.

Living your life to the fullest and making your own decisions doesn't mean you shouldn't take other people's advice into account—it means, simply, make your own decisions. Too many of us default to our parent's dreams for us, or their dreams for themselves, and end up in careers that do not truly play to our strengths and passions. This may lead to many years of unhappiness and an eventual career crisis. If you are not doing what you love right now—even if your dream has been lying dormant since your school or college days—it's time to rethink who or what has stopped you from doing it and decide today what you will do about it.

CHAPTER 6

Que Sera Sera

When I was a little girl,

I asked my mother, what will I be?

Will I be pretty? Will I be rich?

Here's what she said to me

Que sera sera

Whatever will be, will be.

The future's not ours to see.

Que sera sera

As a child my mum used to sing me to sleep with this song. After she died, I lay awake imagining her singing it to me again while I cried myself to sleep every night. Two weeks after her funeral, Emma came to live with me in my student flat in Liverpool. She had no job, and hadn't done well at school, but she didn't want to stay with my dad and Jillian. We slept in the same room, alternating between sleeping on the bed and the floor. I tried to comfort her as best I could, but I'm sure the comfort was meager. I could barely keep up with my own grief.

The flat was always cold and mold grew on the walls around the radiator in the bedroom. In winter the wind howled right through the walls. We cried most of the time and cheered ourselves up with walks to the Albert Docks where we would talk about Mum and buy up fudge meant for tourists. I held a pub job in the evenings and a cleaning job in the mornings to be able to afford the both of us, and I threw myself deep into studies when I wasn't working.

My old flat mates were understanding and tried to protect me from the sad stares when I walked to classes. Had everyone at school heard about my mum? Even acquaintances muttered when I walked past, not knowing what to say or how to act around me. I stopped going to parties and stayed home with Emma unless I had class or work.

Somehow I made it through to graduation the following year. The graduation ceremony came on a warm summer day at the Anglican Cathedral in Liverpool. Proud families bounced around smiling for the camera. It felt like the only mother not in attendance was mine. One of the other dressed up mums walked past me, wearing the aroma of my mum's favorite perfume, Paris by Yves Saint Laurent. The powerful smell memory devastated me. I struggled to keep from crying. When I looked around at all the mothers and daughters it hit me: that would never, ever be me. It was torture, and I vowed someday when I had a daughter, she would never have to go through something like this. I did a lot of faking that day. If you've ever tried faking it, you know it's exhausting and soul destroying. I was tired of faking, and sick to death of this crippling depression.

Following graduation my friends did what nearly everyone does when they come out with a business degree—try to get a job. The "milk round" is a process where big corporations come around the business schools to recruit the best students. They offer corporate graduate training programs and showcase those professional high-paying jobs, like the ones my dad wanted for me. But the thought of the milk round, all the ass kissing, and the ensuing indentured servitude made me sick. I always imagined myself starting my own business, like when I was fourteen, but without money, contacts, or a strong business idea, it wasn't on the cards. So while my friends were spending time on applications and interviewing for jobs, I found myself with a lot of time on my hands, spending much of it in tears with my sister.

I really wanted to get away. I had taken geography classes almost exclusively because I wanted to know all about the world, so I could locate everything out there. Somehow it would help me make sense of what happened with my mum. Life as I knew it was forever changed, like I had turned down a wrong alley, a parallel Twilight Zone universe. I didn't like my direction, and I felt aimless and unprepared for anything. Now seemed like the time to get out, get to where the sun always shines; except, after Mum died, Emma needed me more than ever. Not to mention, there was no money for following dreams.

When all my university friends either left for home or started their new glamorous jobs, I stayed on in Liverpool. Emma and I rented another little flat above a busy local pub in another rough area of Kensington, Liverpool. It was cheap because it was an illegal club playing loud music right up until 2 a.m. I will always remember the boom-boom-boom underneath our floor, being the ceiling of the disco. Our cue for bedtime was the security bouncers repeating to drunken patrons: "Do your talking whilst you're walking!" Time, at last, to get some sleep.

At the end of each night the D.J. played the same song by Charles and Eddie, the lyrics filtering through our floor, a chorus of drunks and underage girls singing along:

Look into my eyes,

Can't you see they're open wide?

Would I lie to you, baby?

Would I lie to you?

Yeah, you lied. I would think. You said you'd always be there for me, Mum.

One New Year's Eve, Emma and I joined them downstairs, dancing around the car park, forcing ourselves to enjoy our freedom. Once everybody else had gone home, we realized we were already home—and miserable.

Thank God I had Emma. Even though we were extremely sad, and neither of us were doing well, we had each other. We blamed Dad, because we had to blame someone else, so we stopped all our contact with him. Emma was as immobilized as I was in deciding what to do with her life; without parental support, without guidance, we drifted. Since I wasn't about to tell her I wanted to travel, we spent another year together.

Eventually, Emma found a job working in the pub downstairs. She started having a social life and coming out of her depression. When she signed up to do some part-time care work at the local hospital, I confided in her at last.

"I need to get out of here," I said. "I want to go traveling. I've saved up some money and I want to buy a ticket and go. What do you think?"

I should have known I didn't have to worry. "Of course, Sam," she said, like her old self. "I'll be okay. I love you and I want you to go see what life is like out there."

The next week, my boyfriend Christopher and I bought 'round the world' tickets for £543 (about $800) on Thai Airways, stopping in London, Delhi, Calcutta, Bangkok, Brisbane, Sydney, Auckland, Wellington, Los Angeles, D.C., and ending back in London. Most people didn't want to do all those stops, including a reluctant Christopher, but I was ready to check out the rest of the world. Best of all, I was going to finally see California.

I had met Christopher my second year at Liverpool while sitting on the floor in the student union, drinking a pint of cider. I looked up and saw this handsome, six-foot-five hippie from Burton-upon-Trent. He was skinny, funny, kind, and we were fast friends. I am grateful for knowing him, and so grateful for his love and support through my mum's tragedy.

Our first stop in India together gave us a heavy dose of culture shock, in a good way. We disembarked the plane, collected our bags, and walked out to the street into our first Delhi traffic jam: three cars, four trucks, a rickshaw, an elephant, a cow, and two more trucks, along with all the men who needed to pee letting loose in the area of the street directly in front of me. I never saw or smelled a stranger thing in my life.

We spent three months in India, traveling up into Nepal and hiking around Annapurna. It was an unforgettable experience. For one thing, kids are everywhere. They come up to you and happily say, "Namaste," a Hindu greeting meaning "I bow to your true self" or "I bow to the divine in you". There are beggars, of course, but mostly they want to meet you and smile at you. The children were very poor, but very happy, and I started to realize how little money one needs to truly enjoy life.

But I was still deeply unhappy and unsettled in my soul. I hadn't finished grieving my mum. My dad and I weren't yet speaking to each other and I missed Emma tremendously. I considered this to be a recovery trip. I thought that if I could get away from home for a while, get out and experience the world, I would be helped through my grief. Along the way, I came to realize that solving immediate problems can take your mind off other problems, letting your subconscious do some of the work; and this was India, so if it could go wrong it certainly would.

Before leaving India, Christopher and I bought bus fare from Katmandu to Calcutta in order to catch our flight to Thailand. We thought we had purchased passage all the way over the border, but somehow were given the wrong tickets. We had already boarded, but were immediately made to get off the bus and walk to the police station. The police questioned us and tried to fine us for not having the correct tickets. We had no way to pay the fine, of course, since we only carried a few pound notes, some change, and our traveler's checks, and it wasn't as though there was an ATM around the corner. They responded by locking us in a jail cell.

Being in jail anywhere is frightening, but being in a jail cell in an Indian village, not speaking the language, nor knowing local customs, and none of your family or friends knowing where in the world you are— that's a real nightmare. With no idea what would happen to us, I did what any self-respecting woman would in such a situation: I burst into tears. Somehow the policemen assessed we weren't hardened criminals or spies and took pity on us. Within a few minutes we were out of jail, another lesson learned. We bought the correct tickets and headed for another bus.

If you have never traveled through India, you may not know that when a bus packed full of people comes along, and by "packed full" I mean like an enormous sardine tin with windows, it means nothing. They will always make room for a few more sardines. You may be asked to stand on the bumper and hang on for dear life or sit on the roof, dodging tree branches, but you can always count on being welcomed aboard with open, if not slightly cramping arms.

"Come on, come on," the driver said, as some of the passengers motioned to us. Christopher climbed up to the roof and I was invited to sit next to the driver at the front of the bus.

The interesting thing about being a woman in situations like this is observing how men honor you as a woman, not out of sexism or superiority, but as a natural reaction to your gender. Some may not care for the idea, but I think it is positive to be honored by anyone, even if it is because of your gender. I felt quite secure; for a little while, anyway.

As we drove off into the night, the passengers settled in. We were scheduled to arrive at the border of India by morning, change some money, and take a train to Calcutta. What could be seen of the mountainous winding road was poorly maintained. What could be seen over the edge of the mountain we were climbing was absolutely nothing. It was a frighteningly long and dark drop.

The passengers were quiet as the road jostled all of us around, still most people slept. I glanced over at the driver who looked terribly tired, like all he wanted was to put the bus on autopilot and climb back with the others for a quick snooze. This worried me, so I began to sing. I not only sang, but waved my arms about like I was directing a choir and looked behind me as though everyone back there would jump in and follow along.

I chose a song Emma and I used to sing as kids on long car trips:

Show me the way to go home.

I'm tired and I want to go to bed.

I had a little drink about an hour ago

And it's gone right to my head.

Some of my fellow passengers glared at me, a mad English tourist interrupting the hypnotic hum of the engine and road noise. I paid no attention. I wasn't interested in what they thought of me.

"Why are you singing?" said the man sitting behind me.

"The driver looks really sleepy and I'm trying to keep him awake," I said.

I'll never forget his reply: "If it is God's will that we die tonight," he said, "it is God's will that we die tonight."

Certainly, a profound way of thinking; if it's your time, it's your time. You can't do anything about it, so live your life to its fullest. What a beautiful Radio Heaven way to look at the world.

Bullshit, I thought. God's will or not, I was twenty-two and not the least bit interested in careening down a mountainside. I faced front deliberately and continued singing. After a while I dozed in and out, still singing, and certain I would save us all. I didn't stop singing until the other sardines were fast asleep, along with the bus driver.

The bus suddenly slid onto the wrong side of the road, waking me instantly. The headlights shone into the rocky face of the sheer drop on the right hand side one moment, then into black nothingness of the left hand side the next, back and forth. I groped for something to steady myself, shouting at the driver, "Wake up! Wake up!"

The driver's eyes opened wide and he gripped the wheel, managing to recover control of the bus and come to a stop on the cliff side of the road.

"My God!" I said, breathless. "That could have been us down there!"

The man I spoke to earlier looked at me, smiled and said, "Your God! See, I told you. It wasn't our time."

He was right, of course, and I deeply misunderstood the wisdom at the time. The fact that certain events in life are meant to be doesn't mean simply resigning ourselves to fate. It means that our actions are always important in the moment but we should feel empowered to live life without fear because we are never truly in power. I tried to control the situation, which was impossible, but I did have an influence. Fate and my actions combined to positively impact the destiny of all on the bus, of that I was sure.

Que sera sera!

The next morning we made it to the border where we thought we'd be able to exchange some traveler's checks, except it happened to be a public holiday so all the banks were closed. We had no Indian money, and by this time we had not eaten in over twelve hours. The train station was a couple of miles away and we had no money for a taxi. A few hours passed and we met some backpackers who offered to let us ride with them and front us our fare until the train station, the only place to change money other than a bank. Only, a few seconds after we took off, one of the wheels on the back of the car fell off. The driver kept going, even as we protested, until he could no longer ignore the problem.

This must be the journey from hell, I thought.

Once the driver changed the wheel we managed to make it to the station, repay our loan, and board the train. The train stopped every few minutes and street kids ran onboard to sell fruit and bottles of lukewarm Coke. I was drooling for one. Christopher and I still only had English money, which no matter how hungry you are, is worthless in India. We found ourselves in the ironic position of begging to beggars.

"You can have this," I said, offering one boy an English pound note, a generous sum to open our negotiations. He laughed. I reached into my pocket and came up with a handful of change, saying, "What about this?"

The boy looked at the pile of foreign change, examining each coin with care. He picked up a shiny, brand new English two-pence; the equivalent of about three cents and said, "I'll take this one."

"No, please take more," I said as I tried to hand him more coins and the pound note, "This is not very much."

"No," he said, with a smile, "this one is gold!" He shoved it in his pocket, handed over a bottle, and walked away down the aisle.

Christopher and I drank like it was the first meal of our lives, filled with gratitude at managing to get a bottle of Coke. Even though we had landed in jail, nearly gone over the side of a cliff, and almost crashed a taxi all within 24-hours, we were aware we were being protected.

That day I sensed a bigger, unseen power for the very first time. The man on the bus introduced me to the idea that life will happen the way it is meant to happen and we will be guided and protected along the way. I saw it when we were released from the jail, when the bus arrived safely, when strangers paid our fare, when we needed our spirits to be fed and received a bottle of Coke to hold us over. Logic may have said otherwise, but in my heart I knew, and I was grateful for the knowledge. With that warmth in my heart, that lukewarm bottle of Coke was the sweetest I had ever tasted.

Ever since that day, this concept has helped me with achieving my goals, and I know it can do the same for you if you let it. Everyone comes at this one differently, but I will say that it is important to tune in to whatever higher power you may believe in and allow it to help you achieve your goals. Maybe there is a greater message behind something that has happened to you, something staring you in the face that you have refused to accept yet.

Que sera, sera. Whatever will be, will be. There is a destiny out there for us all. That is not to say we don't have any control of it. Many of us lose our way on the path of following our true destiny and life feels flat, exhausting, or off purpose. When we find our destined path, life seems easier, it flows, and then help, guidance, and protection appear when they are needed.

Isn't it comforting that we are not alone, that help beyond ourselves is at hand, if only we play our part and follow what is right for us?

What path is it time for you to follow?

CHAPTER 7

Fail Is Not a Four-Letter Word

Failure is an excellent stepping-stone to success. Without failure, we never learn to move out of our comfort zone. The companies seeking the most talented employees deliberately seek those with track records reflecting both failure and success, according to one article in Business Week. Those in the trenches, who have survived their battles and lived to fight another day are blessed with irreplaceable experience and the perseverance born from overcoming hardship.

They are veterans of failure.

I returned to England by way of Australia, Fiji, New Zealand, California and Mexico, and minus my boyfriend Christopher who had said goodbye in Australia, no longer my boyfriend but still a friend. I was 25-years old and, aside from some experience working in restaurants in Australia when the money was tight, I had nothing to return to. No mother, no relationship with my father, no money, and no goals. Even Emma wasn't readily available to me since she had found work as a nanny in Washington D.C. From the sound of her voice on our calls, she was doing much better than I was and having a great time.

Having no goals was tough for me. I had always had goals. I grew more ashamed of my life as the days dragged on. You have a degree, Sam. You could've had a great corporate job right off the bat, Sam. Travelling was a big mistake, Sam. The voice in my head beat me up badly. My confidence at an all-time low. I felt like a total failure.

I arrived back on a cold October evening before the clocks changed. That same evening I arranged to go out with some of my old university friends. I was excited to spend an evening with them, but my excitement died quickly. Soon after we started the party I experienced a real disconnect as they talked about their jobs, their outfits, their boyfriends— all normal topics, to be sure—but tonight they were lackluster. I didn't have anything in common with my university friends now, and we all sensed it.

One of the girls noticed me drifting off into space. "Keep drinking" she said, "It'll make you feel better."

Oh, what the hell, I thought, let's have a party.

At 7 a.m. the next morning I awoke propped up against a wall on the dirty floor of Waterloo Station, alone, with no idea of how I had ended up there. My new coat was gone, and not one of my "friends" was around to watch over me. I sat on the cold cement watching rush hour unfold with a throbbing headache and a somber reality. I had no clue what to do with my life anymore, except to avoid living it.

A smart looking business woman walked past me, looked at me with quick sympathy and put a pound coin in my lap. My all-time low. And did I mention I had never experienced such a headache before? I despised myself for getting so drunk in order to fit in with people who, in the end, could not have cared less about what happened to me at the end of the night. I made my way back to my room and cried myself to sleep. That afternoon, headache in hand, I scoured the newspaper and called all the waitressing jobs I could find. Thankfully, a pub near Buckingham Palace called The Albert hired me to waitress in the restaurant upstairs.

The Albert has operated since 1862 and stands on Victoria Street, a proud contrast to its skyscraper neighbors. It's a jam-packed place most days, with lots of tourists and history seekers and loads of Americans wanting a taste of traditional English fayre before speeding off to sightsee at Buckingham Palace. The hours were long, the pay terrible, and for the next few months my life was what you might call a grind: work, then home, then work, then home. Home wasn't so great either. I was living in a horrible smelly room on the ground floor of an old house in Barons Court. My disappointment in myself, and a little pride, prevented me from speaking to my dad or anyone else to tell them what I was doing. I let everyone think I was fine.

Don't get me wrong, there's nothing wrong with being a waitress, and it led to a number of experiences that never would have happened otherwise, but I struggled with high expectations for myself. I wanted more, but what I wasn't sure. I was tired and too low on confidence to try anything new. You have a business studies degree, came a frequent lecture from the little voice in my head, you should already be doing something normal, what's wrong with you?

One night I came home from the pub to discover my room had been burgled. The only thing of value I had left was my Mum's diamond ring which I had bought back from the pawnshop after selling her Mini Cooper. Oddly enough, that same morning I had one of those gut feelings telling me to hide my money and camera under some clothes on a shelf, but I always wore the ring, so it was safe. The thieves took some clothes, some CDs, and my CD-player but hadn't found the money or camera. I think I must have startled them in the act, because the TV was still there with new dusty handprints all over it, and the back door was swinging open. I crumpled onto the bed and screamed like a crazy woman. Then I cried. Someone above me banged the floor and told me to shut up. I had no insurance and I never called the police.

The next day at the Albert, one of the cooks suggested I try working for a temp agency instead. He said I could earn more money because they were paying closer to £4.50 an hour plus tips, much better than my current £3 an hour. Do the same job for more money? Count me in!

I trudged up to the agency and suitably groveled to the woman inside the office on the high street and she agreed to take me on if I owned a black skirt, white blouse, black bow tie, and agreed to show up at 5 a.m. to wait for possible assignments. She was mean and treated the servers like shit, but my options were scarce, so without much money and no other hope of bettering myself, I took what I had and bought the requisite attire from a thrift-shop down the street.

When I walked into the crowded agency waiting room the following morning, I could see my chances for landing a job were slim. The U.K. had recently joined the European Union and London swelled with workers from all over Europe, apparently all of them wanting to wait tables. That little voice ran amok: Sam, everyone in Europe wants this job, you're not going to get it.

As it turned out, I had no trouble getting hired because along with an open EU came a flood of tourism and plenty of work, as long as you didn't mind working the back-breaking breakfast shift at Hilton London in Hyde Park. Unaccustomed to rising so early at the time, my first instinct was to turn around and crawl right back into bed. I desperately needed the job and wanted to back out of my dead-end, so I tried to reclaim my old habit of doing the best job I could, even if I didn't love it. I forced a smile, and set out for the hotel.

It was a long first day. During slow times on the floor, as the staff waited for the next wave of guests, I organized the breakfast buffet and cleaned the floor rather than stand around talking or smoking cigarettes out back. I figured the day would go by faster if I stayed busy. By the end of my first shift, somebody had noticed.

"You look like you know what you're doing," another waitress said to me. "They are looking for full-time people here, the tips are good because there's lots of Americans. You'd be perfect." A nice enough compliment, but I had gotten the agency job and thought I should stick with it, until she added: "Oh, and if you get the job, they give you a room, so you don't have to pay rent somewhere else."

Okay, now we're talking. Immediately, I took a deep breath and paced downstairs to the restaurant manager's office.

"Anita told me you were looking for people," I said, "would you be open to me applying?"

He looked me up and down with a little skepticism and finally said, "Sure."

The next day, I had a new full-time job with decent hours, a clean new room to stay in, and better pay. The restaurant sat directly opposite Hyde Park and catered to American tourists who wanted directions to sightseeing and fun activities. They also rewarded sightseeing information and accurate directions with American sized tips.

It made me want to live in America even more. They were all so friendly, happy, and rich!

After a week on the job, the manager came to me and said, "You're really good at this. We'd like to make you a supervisor, if you're interested." He said being a supervisor would be tough, the tips were less, and the position had a high turnover for good reason. On the other hand, I'd be on a real career-track with more potential and be able to choose my shifts.

I accepted. I could sense the difference in playing to my strengths right away. I started to feel good about myself again. Feeling good is important, but feeling the fulfillment of our potential and working within our aptitudes is more important and leads to even more enjoyment in business. I loved working at Hilton. It helped me realize I enjoyed training people. It became deeply satisfying to witness people grow and develop and learn a skill and I could have a hand in their growth.

When Hilton sent me to a customer-service skills training course led by two professional corporate trainers, little did I realize that my life was about to take another new turn. I sat mesmerized, watching the corporate trainers do their work. It looked like the coolest job in the world. I imagined myself at the front of the room, training, teaching, helping people. It was a defining moment for me and the first time I had ever hit on something that gave me vision and excited me for the future. This wasn't only a job to earn money, but a potential career where I could find fulfillment.

It is a great moment when you realize this is what I want to do. And it was important to pay attention to my feelings about this idea, and not let the little voice in my head shoot it down. I had no idea how to be a corporate trainer; I had no idea how to get the skills or the experience; but I didn't let it stop me from believing that it was possible. I told myself I would find a way to do it and I knew that as long as I kept the goal alive, a way would be found.

I transferred from Hyde Park to Hilton Wembley, a hectic hotel catering to football matches and concerts at the nearby stadium. It was a high pressure location which forced me to develop top notch organizational skills in order to manage it well and was an extraordinary learning experience.

I remember one unusually busy breakfast shift on a Sunday morning. Three servers hadn't shown up for work and I needed help, badly, or we weren't going to make it through the shift. It was 6 a.m. and the general manager, staying overnight, was asleep upstairs in his room.

Who is he to be sleeping? I thought, he's the general manager and it's his hotel falling to pieces, but my head in the noose if these people start leaving from the poor service. I must have talked to myself all the way to his room, because when I looked up, I stood right in front of him in his doorway, wearing pyjamas and scratching his head.

"I need help."

"You could have called on the phone," he grunted.

But I had done exactly what he wanted someone in my position to do—ask for help. I was promoted again.

I worked for Hilton for a few more years, but I wanted something more. Eventually, my experience landed me an even better job at the well-known Smollensky's On The Strand restaurant in the center of London.

It's important to recognize the specific activities we love and where we excel, and to take note of any distinctions between the two. While I was good at running restaurants, I didn't love it, but I was also good at developing people and I loved it. I had discovered my magic mixture, and it was critically important to realize it. My job as a restaurant manager gave me some opportunities for training, but it wasn't nearly enough for my goals. I was determined to find a way to get the right experience and the right skills.

One quiet Monday evening at The Strand, while leafing casually through a hospitality industry magazine, I found my way. There was an advertisement seeking corporate trainers for a well-known cruise line. I remember the wording exactly: "Wanted, Corporate Trainers – Travel in The Caribbean, Europe, Alaska, USA." This is what I had waited for. It couldn't be more perfect. My two favorite activities, training and traveling, all wrapped up in a single dream job. I couldn't yet imagine what the hefty pay-raise would mean to my standard of living.

I ripped out the ad and put it in my coat pocket.

You would think with such a clear sign, so much internal motivation, confidence in my working assets at an all-time high, and a new vision of what my future could become that I would have applied for the job that very minute, but something stopped me. That nagging little voice that questioned my level of experience, whether I was good enough, or if I would make a fool of myself. The little voice that said I couldn't leave London, that I had commitments. I had a boyfriend, an older man who had "separated" from his wife and was "trying" to leave her, although I didn't believe him, but I continued to see him. Luckily for me, he abruptly stopped returning my calls one day, releasing me to pursue my dream job.

I rifled through my coat pockets and found the wrinkled piece of paper, the deadline had passed by a full month. I called anyway, and to my delight they hadn't filled the position. I found my resume, sent it off with a cover letter and was accepted for an interview. I was informed that for the interview I would be required to make a presentation about why I wanted to work with the cruise line and any ideas I had about training. I would need slides.

Yes, slides.

This was long before PowerPoint, so these slides were of the overhead projector variety, the expensive kind you have to get professionally printed. I found myself spending more than I could afford on another possibility. So what? I wanted this job.

I did intense research, learning everything I could about the cruise line and their business model. Being passionate about the company would go a long way during the interview, even if I didn't know much about the job itself. Impressing hiring managers is easy when you take the time to get to know the company. You can be fairly sure they prefer hiring interested people who are excited to work for them. I created the slides in color which cost me £67 (about $100) to print, a fortune at the time. During the interview I was forthright that I had no experience as a corporate trainer, but my experience in hospitality, my presentation, and my passion for training must have shone through.

They hired me!

The next thing I knew, my first day of work in Miami, Florida arrived. My life seemed more complete than in a very long time. Yes, I had failed, but what a way to bounce back even higher than before. I also had a solid corporate job like my university friends—correction—not like them, better than them. I was finally in America, basking in the Miami sun. I hadn't taken the job for the money, instead I was doing exactly what I wanted because I had persevered, recognized my skill set, and finally risen off my backside to do something about it.

The job was a dream come true, until I met my manager. Tracy was a political queen. My new Irish friend and fellow trainee, Orla, and I could never understand how Tracy wormed her way into any job managing people. She didn't care about people, at least not us people. She cared more about playing politics and kissing up to her American boss who thought she was great because all he ever saw was her ass kissing smoke-screen, not her management ability.

Like Aileen Mersh, my bully from the council estate, Tracy firmly disliked me and had no problem letting me know.

During my first performance review, Tracy bragged, "You know, the trouble with you, Sam, is you think you're better at this than me."

Well, that's because I am! I thought.

Most of the time she was nice to my face, but behind my back her personal mission was to get me fired. She often used the power of her position to make my work life as miserable as possible, giving me odd projects, assigning me to do other people's work, even attempting to isolate me from other employees she suspected I liked or who she knew were my friends. This backfired because, as with everyone who had the misfortune of working with her, our mutual dislike of Tracy was our bond.

In spite of Tracy's efforts, the cruise line gave me the enviable assignment of joining a team to bring a brand new ship over from Italy to New York and overseeing the training of the crew. In the cruise line business, being entrusted with a transatlantic crossing of any kind is a big deal, but to be given a brand new ship, the largest liner in the world at the time, spoke volumes about their faith in me. If Tracy wanted me fired, she was going to need help.

I could say Tracy was a poor teacher, I suppose, but the truth is I learned a lot from her. I learned to keep a notepad with me at all times and I wrote down every time she treated someone poorly. The list of don'ts she generated for my list was a long one: don't be mean, don't be political, don't commit and not follow through, don't be dishonest, don't treat people like they're dumb, don't harass, and many others. I knew that someday, when I had my own business, these would become solid material for my policies. For now, they were training.

The most important lesson I learned from Tracy was that when you do a job you're not cut out for—only for the money, or the power, or another dysfunctional reason—you will hate yourself and probably force others to hate you along the way. Paying attention to what you enjoy doing most and building your career around it is critical to true success.

When I arrived in Italy, the ship wasn't ready to sail. It was still under construction and, according to the foreman, would be for another three weeks. I'd have had no problem lounging around a luxury cruise liner for three weeks all by myself, but I wasn't alone, there were around 900 other crew members whose training was to take place en route. There we all were, stuck on a big ship outside a tiny town a few hours from Venice with nothing to do except shore leave. Everything looked like it would be fine until the governor of this tiny town came onboard the ship to inform us no one could leave until his office checked everyone's passports and papers, and it would take three to five days.

As the corporate trainer, my job became to create an entertaining at-mosphere for the crew. We opened up the bar, played bingo, and gener-ally tried to make it fun, and it was a wild scene; a 24-hour party with a crew who knew how to party.

One evening, hanging out at the crew bar, the cigarette smoke grew so thick I could barely see. My eyes started stinging and hurting badly. I needed some drops to soothe my eyes, but since there was no medical staff yet on board, I asked around if anyone could get me something from the pharmacy in town.

One of the crew told me about "this one guy" who had been here longer than everyone else. He came to work in the casino to install the slot machines. His name was Steven, he was smart, and he might be able to get me off the ship. I walked down a couple of levels into the casino and, sure enough, there was a guy working there. His hair was black, longish and curly, he had a cool little beard on his chin and deep, dark eyes. He was Canadian, but looked remarkably Italian. I could care less where he was from, he was gorgeous.

I introduced myself and explained the situation. As I kept talking, I sensed some attraction. He felt it, too, judging from his eagerness to help. He had a special pass and he could get us off the ship, and he wanted to meet up around 10 a.m. the next morning. Sounded good to me.

The next morning I turned up to meet Steven in my favorite dress with the yellow sunflowers. We walked the short distance into town and ate ice cream before going into the pharmacy for the eye drops. We had an instant connection with one important passion in common: a love of life on the run.

Steven was from a small town in Canada and couldn't wait to get out and travel the world. He was your stereotypical good-looking-bad-boy with swagger; the one who would never managed to be tamed by a woman. He had a reputation, but so did I, and it became my personal mission to domesticate this wild beast. I rather liked his controversial views and aversion to the ways of the world, and he liked me. We were both bored with being trapped on the ship, and so a relationship was born, the first serious one in a long time for either of us.

On the ship, Steven lived in a tiny uncomfortable crew-cabin below deck. Since my position entitled me to a nice guest cabin with windows, a rare commodity on a cruise ship, it made perfect sense for him to move in. We spent every night of the remaining three weeks together while workmen completed the ship, then we sailed to New York. When the Twin Towers of New York came into view, and the ship arrived to a fanfare of press, helicopters, and thousands of guests awaiting us at port, I imagined it was all for us.

Quickly after, we were assigned to other ships, but kept connected through phone calls and emails; both especially difficult as service is hard to come by on a cruise ship and we were not allowed personal use of email. We managed, though somehow it was mostly me who initiated the emails and calls, waiting longingly for his slow and slight replies.

Tracy was still after me, but as long as I stayed squeaky clean and did my job professionally, she couldn't touch me. My training skills grew and my confidence skyrocketed. I was now a seasoned traveler and I wanted to see it all, so I volunteered for every possible cruise and tried to get on whatever ships I could to visit Steven as often as possible.

Going from ship to ship was lonely and completely impractical for a healthy romantic relationship. Doubts often crept in as to Steven's faithfulness. I was also growing dissatisfied with the job, the politics presenting more challenges than ever. I couldn't envision myself progressing up this particular corporate ladder, feeling like I might not fit in. Inexplicably, desires to start my own business fired off in my mind and, as much as I tried to quench them, I couldn't ignore them.

I buried my head in work, setting a goal to do every cruise they offered and visit as many countries as I could. I travelled the entire Caribbean and Hawaiian Islands, and some of South America and Canada. I was also extremely pleased to go to Los Angeles, and work the cruises to Mexico and Catalina Island. California at last! I had missed it since my visit after college and I enjoyed every moment while I was there.

Then two and a half years after starting with the cruise line, I was finally assigned to the Alaska cruise, the only ship and cruise I hadn't worked by then—and the one I wanted most. I set up a new crew-training center on the ship out of Alaska, and I felt that I made a real difference to the crew and the training systems. You might even say it was my crowning glory, and I fully expected to return to the Miami home office to a fanfare.

It was not so. Tracy found some fault or other in my work and relocated me to a ship in the Southernmost Caribbean as a punishment. What she didn't know was that my romance with Steven was still in full infatuation mode, and he was stationed there. Revenge was sweet.

My job on the ship, which was docked in Puerto Rico, was setting up a crew-training center and managing programs for customer service, management, and basic English. I was really in my element now, because this crew came from all over the world—South America, the Philippines, Africa, Russia— and there was a lot of English to be taught and I loved every minute. I thought I'd finally made it at twenty-nine-years-old with a great corporate job on a cruise line, traveling the world, training interesting people, and madly in love. Life was good.

I even started working on my Master's degree in Training and Human Resource Management by distance learning with the University of Leicester in the U.K. I loved writing essays sitting on the top deck, out in the sun on quiet days in port while the crew and passengers were off exploring the Caribbean towns and beaches. It was like having the boat all to myself.

Steven and I ended up sharing my cabin together again. Technically, the rules forbade unmarried people living together, but since many in the crew did it, everyone turned a blind eye to the rule.

Everyone but Tracy.

One day at port in Puerto Rico, she paid a surprise visit to the ship and during the first day somehow found out about Steven staying in my cabin. She cut short her inspection and hauled me back to Miami for a disciplinary hearing. There was no getting around it. She had me.

Damn.

I knew Tracy was after me. She had already managed to get my friend Orla fired, and she would regularly perform back flips attempting to get to me. While I was a good girl who never did anything wrong she couldn't touch me, but in the end, all she needed to do was sit back and wait for me to hand her the grounds, all wrapped up with a bow on top.

The day of the hearing I was called in to see Tracy's superior.

"We have to let you go," he said, "you've done exemplary work, but we can't overlook this. We'll give you the option to take a three-month sabbatical, and you can decide to not come back." A political way of firing me without making it public, having me make the decision. Of course, I agreed.

I was gutted. Failure again. I completely messed up my dream job. Both scared and worried, I blamed Tracy, I blamed the cruise line. I wallowed through a private pity party for days. They wanted me to leave straight away, so I packed up my case and boarded a plane to Heathrow. I phoned Emma to ask if I might be able to stay with her for a few weeks. I had less than £1,000 (about $1,500) in my bank account, no place to live, and three months to replace my job. Thank goodness for Emma, now a live-in nanny in North London, who asked her employers if I could stay in her room for a while. They said it would be fine for a few weeks. At least my housing was taken care of, temporarily.

Surprisingly, Steven gave his notice at the cruise line and promised to be in England within a few weeks. I took this as a sign of his true love for me. I had him, but what about my derailed career-track?

It's hard to go back to the January cold of London after living in cruise-liner temperatures for so long. Instead of a comfy cabin suite, I slept on Emma's floor with all my belongings in a bag beside me. I had hit bottom again, but I hustled and started looking at job applications and agencies. I was determined to use those three months to land an even better job and to prove to my old bosses that they were doing me a favor. The trouble was no other job I applied for seemed to fit me. I tried out a couple of recruitment agencies and endured the usual third-degree, but it still felt wrong. I over-ate and was unable to get up off my bed, which was still the floor.

Failure is one of the bitterest pills you can swallow. I was, in some sick way, enjoying wallowing in the difficulty and pain of my almighty fall. I kept thinking I was a big fraud all along, and this was the real me, so why bother?

One day I found myself listlessly searching through internet job postings. I turned on the radio and Every Breath You Take by The Police came on:

Every move you make,

Every vow you break,

Every smile you fake,

Every claim you stake,

I'll be watching you.

Mum told me once that this was her song dedicated to me. She really was watching me. Thank you, Radio Heaven.

I listened to the song, and suddenly heard an old familiar voice inside me saying "What if this failure is the best thing ever to happen to you? What if, in actuality, there is no such thing as failure, only learning?"

This is potentially an opportunity, I told myself, because the corporate world is not really your bag is it, Sam? You didn't do a good job playing politics and making nice with your boss!

I learned a lot from my job on the cruise line, I really did. If I had wanted it more, I could have played the game, but the reality was that career, and that life, was not the one for me.

I imagine everyone is scared of failing when it comes to going after their big goals and dreams; however, I also knew—though I resisted it to begin with—that I needed only to ask myself, "What's the worst that can happen if you fail?"

My work with the cruise line revealed my passion for developing people, helping them make the most of their lives, their potential, and their talents. Seeing a spark in their eyes was important and inspiring. With new momentum, I acknowledged the unknown. I had no idea what my company could do other than training, coaching, and developing people in some way—but for what?

The lesson here is to learn to embrace failure, and see it as a stepping-stone on the way to your success. Failing is an inevitable part of creating your destiny. Now, I welcome it. After learning to deal with disappointment, I knew persistence and dedication to my goals would eventually be rewarded.

What can you learn from your failures? If nothing else, I hope you realize failure is temporary and failure is good even if, undeniably, it feels like shit when it happens. When something goes wrong, we need to learn to say, "Something good is happening here." (A saying I would learn from my future husband!) Look for the greater message of the experience and expect it to, eventually, turn out for the good. Recognizing this will come more easily with practice.

I heartily recommend routine failing. It means you are actually active, doing something, moving forward. Too often we buy into what society says, or what the past has shown us, is going to work or not work. When we do that, we limit ourselves. I also highly recommend losing at least one job in your life because it gives you awareness and an aliveness you don't get when you have the same job for life. It forces you to tune in to what you truly want in a career.

For me, it tuned me in to what I wanted and how I could play to my strengths; to what was needed from me in the world, and to what I could provide to fulfill the needs of others. The tricky part is doing this without being paralyzed by the mass of fears or listening to the negative voices creeping in around you. I was struggling with little money, my sister as my only support in London, no network, and no solid business idea, and who on earth was I to think I could create one out of thin air?

I had three months to find out.

CHAPTER 8

Poker Face

Poker, like life, is a game of strategy, not merely luck. While the outcome of any particular hand involves significant chance, there is always one winner in a round. The long-run expectation of the players, as determined by their actions, is chosen on the basis of probability, psychology of other players, and game theory. It's important in poker to take intelligent, calculated risks—not crazy, but strategic risks—and then patiently and calmly wait for the results.

This was something Steven taught me.

Poker was a life-long passion Steven inherited from his grandfather. With my family history and fears around money, honestly, it scared me; but, I also loved his anti-establishment attitude and the "Wow. How cool." response people always gave to hearing that he played professional poker. Poker played to Steven's strengths, an I.Q. through the roof and great bluffing skills. Steven had always wanted to live in England, and now he wanted to try his hand as a professional player in some of London's best casinos. That was his new job.

My job was to find an apartment. There wasn't room on Emma's floor for another person, so we needed a cheap place to rent. I found a small, newly built flat by the train station in West Ham, East London. It would be easy for us both to get in and out and was close to the city and everything we would need. However, when Steven arrived a few weeks later, he was adamant that the proximity of a nearby cell phone tower would interrupt his brain waves and immediately wanted to move, even though I had already paid a deposit and moved in. In fact, he obsessed over any device with even the slightest potential to interrupt brain activity. Steven was unusual, but love was blind, and I agreed to forfeit our deposit and move again.

This time, he took over the apartment search and came up with an awful hole-in-the-wall in Ilford in Essex, a second-floor apartment above a house. The furniture was old and full of holes, the floors were dirty, and the smell of curry hit you hard as you walked through the door. Don't get me wrong, I love curry as much as any other red-blooded Englishwoman, but this place reeked of an old stale curry, the smell sticking to every object in the house. But, at least, it wasn't anywhere near a cell phone tower. Dutifully, I moved in and cleaned it as best I could.

We do that, don't we? We sacrifice ourselves and say okay to people because we don't want them to be upset, even if it means taking actions we might never do otherwise. What can I say? My love-blinders were planted firmly over my eyes.

Steven had little or no interest in me, going off every night to play poker and sleeping through the day. I lost almost all confidence, descending further into my sadness because I couldn't bring myself to blame Steven. At bedtime, I mastered the art of silently crying into my pillow so I wouldn't disturb the neighbors below. The mascara left on my pillowcases was the only sign, which Steven never saw because I laundered them each morning.

It wasn't the on-land relationship I desired, but I did what I had always done under pressure, put my head down and focused on work.

If I wanted to start my own business, I would have to network. The trouble was I disliked networking tremendously as it always seemed fake. Oh, who am I kidding? The truth is networking made me nervous. How would I even answer the question: "What do you do?"

I dragged myself to a women's networking event one evening, hiding in the bathroom until the speaker arrived. Women came in and out without notice until Melissa introduced herself as I pretended to wash my hands for the fiftieth time. She was an executive with a private bank in the city and said she didn't like networking either. I had found my people! I relaxed enough to leave the bathroom and sit with her. Little did I realize the role she would soon play in my life.

#

Since Steven slept during the day and "worked" at the casino at night, we rarely spent time together. But the clock ticked away on my deadline, so I spent a lot of time walking around London, thinking over what my new business would be. I remember sitting in a little church garden on Liverpool Street right in the heart of London's financial district. I shivered, wrapped up in layers, on a little churchyard bench, and watching all kinds of activity going on around me. A throng of City workers hurried to their offices, London cabs honked, the imposing skyscrapers hummed with activity, and the little garden was like an oasis of peace amidst the chaos.

I watched the scene carefully, struck by the number of men compared to the scarcity of women. Sitting there, I noticed something else about the women. I saw one younger woman zip by incredibly fast with two kids in a stroller, another woman power-walked in an immaculate suit trying to get somewhere quickly, and yet another ran full speed barking instructions to her nanny through a cell phone. Each woman was in a hurry, and each looked completely stressed.

These were all powerful and successful women who reminded me of my mum in her power suit days. I was impressed at what they had achieved and I wanted to be like them. I couldn't help but wonder if they were happy, or if they were secretly faking it like my mum did for all those years—outwardly successful, inwardly depressed. Did they hate networking, too? Probably not, they looked so confident.

The real question was whether these successful women were balanced and fulfilled, as well as successful? Work/life balance, I thought, that's important, isn't it? I could start a business to help women develop skills to balance a career and a satisfying life, squeezing everything good out of both without leaving them stressed-out and unhappy.

I recognized that I could be on to something. At the very least, I sensed I was close, because the energy of inspiration bubbled up, warming me from the inside as I sat shivering by myself in a church garden, terrified and excited at the same time. Where to begin? I came up with the bones of an idea: a work/life balance event for women in London. Not exactly a full-scale plan, but the seed of an idea was emerging. As the notion took root in my brain, I came up with even more ideas, but I also made war with all my gremlins over them.

And it was then I began an essential habit: pulling weeds.

Inspiration is a lot like keeping your garden in shape. We have to pluck the negative mental weeds that pop up when we first think of something in order to allow the healthy growth of the inspired idea. It will take shape all on its own, but only if we allow it. Pulling the weeds isn't easy, I know. The temptation to allow negative thoughts to take over is a strong one. If we let them grow unchecked, the weeds will take over completely, but if we want the idea to grow to its fullest potential, we must pull those weeds!

As I left the churchyard and walked, I had a little conversation with myself:

I can't do an event because I don't know anybody.

"Let's keep going on with the idea for a moment, Sam." I said out loud. "Let's say you can do an event on work/life balance, what would it look like? Have a look at all these women around you in the City. Really look at them. What would they like to have in an event based on work/life balance?"

Well, they would like to come to a nice setting and be served good food and drinks... Champagne!

"So far, so good!"

And they would like to meet other like-minded women with whom they can share their experiences and learn from each other.

"Excellent!"

They would also like to learn about managing their home and career life, and to build new skills.

My plan started taking on a life of its own. When I finished having this exchange with myself, and nearly ready to take the project on with full conviction, I looked up to see a five star hotel, newly renovated and beautiful, right in front of me.

This should do for my venue!

I walked into the lobby and was in awe of the sweeping staircase and the traditional features combined with a modern edge. I walked out and back in a few times before I finally mustered the courage to go to the reception desk and ask for the general manager. I knew something about how hotels worked from my years at Hilton and thought I would try something out. After waiting a while, the duty manager walked up and introduced himself.

"This is a gorgeous hotel!" I said.

He looked at me, smiling politely, unable to tell if I was selling something. I was dead serious, despite the delivery—this gorgeous hotel would make women feel special, a posh place to learn about work/life balance.

"I imagine, since you're a new hotel," I said, knowing all new hotels need to bring in new business any way they can, "you're going to want to bring in a lot of good people."

"Yes, of course," he said.

"So, if I were to bring twenty high-flying women of the City into your hotel for an evening event, would you give me a conference room for free?" It was a daring question, but I had made harder requests of more difficult people, and I had nothing to lose by asking.

He paused thoughtfully and said, "You'd have to pay for food and drinks, of course; but yes, we'd be happy to give you a conference room if you bring twenty high-flying women from the City into our hotel."

"Thank you," I said coolly, avoiding any temptation to get down on the floor and kiss his feet, "may I have a look at the room?"

The conference room was beautiful; light streamed in through enormous Victorian windows onto an all-white, exceptionally modern decor. The huge conference room would be perfect. I booked the date for two months out on a Tuesday evening.

As I headed back to our stinky little flat, I had new energy in my stride... Look at me, everyone! I thought. I'm doing an event for twenty high-flying women of London. They'll drink champagne and have delicious food and I'm going to talk about work/life balance, or find somebody to talk about work-life balance, because what do I know about work/life balance? But here I am creating my very own business! I sensed a wonderfully intoxicating combination of excitement, mixed with an enormous amount of fear—a combination of emotions I'd reference from then on as the litmus test of a good idea, and what I now refer to as my Vision Test.

I called Emma and she came over to celebrate.

"You need an office," she said.

So we created my first company office in front of the window in the living room of the stinky flat. Emma put a red scarf over the table to brighten it up, and even brought over a wire magazine rack to serve as my filing cabinet. We then realized I had no office chair, so we walked up the high street to Argos and made the first official business purchase, a black office chair with wheels to zoom around hard floors. We carried the flat pack back home and assembled the chair together. I did a lot of great work in my chair, and I still have it to this day.

Still in my Master's degree program, I enrolled in a coaching training program to enhance the skills I developed on the cruise line. The first weekend course, one of my fellow students told me she had recently received her MBA, specializing in women and work/life balance. Naturally, I asked her if she would present her research at the event and she said yes!

I had a room. I had a speaker. Now all I needed was the twenty high-flying women of London. I still didn't have any business contacts in the city, not really, so I started to panic. Suddenly, the challenge of finding twenty women, out of the millions of women in the city, seemed insurmountable. The little voice I worked so hard to ignore returned with a vengeance, weeds quickly began to sprout. What on earth were you thinking? This is crazy. How will you, Sam Collins, get successful women to come to an event presented by a total stranger?

I let the panic happen, and guess what? It subsided after a while.

After resigning to a more positive outlook, I said to myself, "There has to be a way. Let's get creative in thinking about this. I committed to running this event for whoever these twenty high-flying women of London are. Only two problems: first, nobody knows about the event, and second, nobody knows Sam Collins."

No one would come to an event presented by Sam Collins, but that didn't mean they wouldn't come to an event presented by a company with an impressive sounding name. I still needed to come up with one. At first, I thought I should call my company "Y-Coach." I shared this idea with Emma during an impromptu brainstorming session.

"Hey, Y not?"

Thankfully, Emma came up with something better: "If somebody is looking you up in the Yellow Pages and your company begins with Y," she said, "you'll be right at the end. Call it something beginning with A and you'll be right at the top." The year was 2000, back in the old days when people used telephone directories, not Google.

"Brilliant, Emma," I said. "A really good point!" I randomly picked up a magazine sitting on the coffee table in the curry flat to look for inspiration. As soon as I flipped it open, a single word leapt off the page: Aspire. Emma and I looked it up in our little English dictionary on the book shelf.

Aspire: To have a great ambition or ultimate goal, desire strongly; to strive toward an end; to soar.

"I LOVE IT!" I said, tingling all over as I imagined an entire future all wrapped up in my new company name. "That's exactly it!"

As the Founder and CEO of newly created Aspire, my first order of business was creating a website with an event page for purchasing tickets. I knew nothing about websites, but Martin, Head Pastry Chef at the fancy hotel, did web design on the side; since he was just starting out he offered to set it up for free, and he still manages the Aspire websites today.

My next executive decision was finding a way to market the event. I reached out to the only people I knew in London at the time: my sister, her employer, my former boss from Hilton, and Melissa, the banker from the bathroom. I wrote my only email invitation to my mailing list of four, asking if they would please pass it on to their female friends and colleagues who might be interested in attending. The cost was £45 to cover the expenses of food and the champagne.

I clicked 'Send', sat back, and waited.

And waited.

Each day I checked my email, each day there was no response. Two weeks later, I had a grand total of zero high-flying women of the City signed up to my event.

There is a limit to how many weeds you can pull in a two-week period, and I couldn't hold it back any longer. The little voice started to run rampant and tell me all the reasons—with visible proof this time—why this was all such a stupid idea.

Okay, I thought, as near to surrender as I have ever been, it isn't meant to be. I envisioned groveling back to the cruise line and Tracy, or some other corporate job, or another restaurant. I started to think my crazy dream was just that—crazy.

Depressed and deflated, I phoned Melissa.

"If you haven't sent out that e-mail yet," I said, "then don't worry about it."

"Oh!" she said. "Sorry, I sent it out today."

"Well, how many people did you send it to?" I asked.

"Everyone I know," she said. "Including our banking women's network. I asked them to send it on, too. So, a few thousand, maybe."

A few thousand? What was worse, no one signing up, or the potential of a few thousand?

"Well, I really appreciate it," I said, forcing some positivity into my voice, "Let's see what happens." Inside I was terrified. I would only embarrass myself and fail completely again. I barely slept that night. The next afternoon when I logged into my computer, I prepared myself for the worst.

I couldn't believe what I saw. Four signups. But rather than hope, my heart sank deeper. Oh, God! I thought, slapping my laptop closed, it's even worse than none. I can't do a big event with only four women. Now I'm going to have to tell them it's not happening. This is going to be really embarrassing, least of all to me... now I'm going to embarrass Melissa, too.

I put off making a decision. A few tense hours dragged by as I strategized how I might get out of this thing. I checked my email again.

What the hell? Nine people.

The next day it was sixteen.

As the days progressed, the numbers kept going up.

My fears were completely dispelled, my jumping conclusions settled, and even better, the impulse to fulfill my dream was on its way to being amply rewarded. In the end, the first Aspire event hosted not four, not sixteen, or even twenty; we hosted 150 high-flying women of the City.

Thank goodness the room was so big!

Seeing the power of women willing to help each other was fantastic. Women can and do help other women succeed. Women who were total strangers to me had received an email from a friend and passed it on to their friends, whether they could attend or not, to help spread the word. It changed my life, and I am forever grateful to them all.

It also proved that there is power at work in goal setting. Lacking all the traditional ingredients for business success—a huge network, lots of money, experience, everything in place ahead of time—I discovered I could start a business without them, or pick them up along the way. Passion, purpose, and a good heart can get you there.

Oh, and a little patience doesn't hurt!

Results don't always come immediately, so we must train ourselves to temper negative thoughts. Negative thoughts are, anyway, only thoughts. Usually, they don't do much besides reinforce further negativity, being generated from fear rather than reality. If I had believed the story in my head, that no women would show up, or that Melissa would be embarrassed, or I would be embarrassed in front of Melissa, I would have had 150 cancellations instead of one of the greatest victories of my working career and the founding of a marvelous career journey to follow.

The first Aspire event turned out wonderfully. I was very nervous as I had never spoken to such a large group before. Despite all my training experience, I came out in itchy red hives right before my big introduction. Emma tied a scarf around my neck to hide them and told me to ease up on the lipstick, since I had worn the kind that cakes up and goes crusty the more you apply.

I took a deep breath and reflected that I wouldn't have to go groveling back to the cruise line, or work a corporate job, or play by somebody else's rules for the rest of my life. That night, I obtained my first coaching clients and made a life-long friend of a Human Resources Director from Disney named Gillian, who stayed behind at the end, drinking whiskey and smoking.

Aspire would not exist today if I hadn't taken these risks, stayed on course, and refused to listen to the negative thoughts and comments from myself and others. Some people told me you can't start a business unless you have seed money, unless you have a network, unless you are a certain age, unless, unless, unless. Some well-intentioned people indeed said, "You're way too young to start your own business, especially in the coaching, consulting, and training type field. You need to be at least forty, and you have to have a pedigree and experience. Why risk it when success is so unlikely?"

When I said, "I want to specialize in working with women," it threw people for another loop.

Again, people tried to throw water on the flame: "You'll alienate men and people will think you're a feminist, which will never work in the business world. Business is a man's world, Sam, it won't work."

Steven, who I looked to for support, wasn't any help either, saying, "You're too nice to be in business, you can't make money and be nice." If I had bought in to all the negativity, then I would never have taken those risks. I would never even have started Aspire, and never written a doctoral thesis, let alone this book.

Many of us buy in to someone else's absolute bullshit about what should or could or would be, influenced to stop following our own dreams. It's such a shame. It's a shame on all of us. We need to realize that its complete rubbish, particularly us women. Society says we should be the perfect mother, a supermodel, and Wonder Woman. We should do everything, except this, be everything, except that. It's absolutely crazy, especially in the Western world today.

Take a leap, take calculated risks, and be patient for the results. We don't need to have everything worked out beforehand. I never wrote a business plan, but in order to reach the next level in life, business, and my own personal growth, I had to take some risks.

Perhaps there is a leap of faith you have put off making; a risk it's time for you to take. Focusing intently upon the people you want to work with or impact, and what they need most from you, is often the best prod to get you taking some risks. It gets you out of your head and into your gut instinct pretty quickly and successfully.

CHAPTER 9

The Unhappiest Day of My Life

"We should probably get married," Steven said one night a few weeks before my first Aspire event, "what do you think?"

"I think that was so romantic. No."

"I mean, seriously," he said, leaning over to me, softening his voice. "I mean it sort of makes sense, right? My visa's running out. And I love you. I don't cheat on you. What's the problem?"

"No problem here," I said.

"Seriously," he said, looking serious, "I don't cheat on you, and I've cheated on everyone else. That means you're special."

"Okay," I said, not feeling very special somehow.

"And I promise you this: we will have a big wedding in Las Vegas later in the year, something really amazing."

That was my marriage proposal. Not the most romantic, like our apartment, but by then I knew Steven well; for him it was equivalent to saying something positively Shakespearean. It was entirely up to me to translate it into English. In Steven's world, if he wasn't cheating, you were special. I lived in Steven's world and this was high praise.

There was no engagement ring. He said we didn't need them because they were a meaningless symbol. Funnily enough I had always assumed you wear a symbol because it means something. He had gone bust in the casino the night before, so we didn't have the money to buy one anyway.

Despite all this, I awoke on my wedding day happy because there was something else about the night of the first Aspire event—it was also the night before my wedding. At the end of the event I announced to the crowd it was my Hen Night (British for bachelorette party) and many of them stayed late with me for drinks at the bar. Somehow it felt normal to be celebrating my marriage to a professional poker player with a bunch of strangers at a business event—who was judging?

I didn't have appropriate wedding attire, so I popped down the street in the morning and bought a white-ish wedding-ish blouse and remembered I had some black trousers at home that would complete the outfit. I reminded myself this wasn't an official wedding, and we would have some real fun in Vegas, baby! But I have to admit, I was still feeling romantic.

Emma, with her new Nigerian boyfriend David, would serve as our witnesses and met us at the tube train to Highgate, where we had scheduled our appointment with the judge. We came off the tube at Tottenham High Road and ran into an Accessorize shop to buy rings. Two rings at £5 each, just so we would have something. Steven suggested we use rubber bands, in his world this was called humor.

Steven kept calling it a formality and wondered aloud why I was so dressed up. I practically forced him into a suit and tie because in my eyes, it was still our wedding day.

Steven did not see the world through my eyes.

My stomach growled as we waited. I was a bit hung over from drinking after the event, fighting waves of nausea and a swimming headache. Suddenly I thought, What are you doing, Sam? You shouldn't be getting married. This isn't right at all!

"It's pre-wedding jitters," I said quietly, summarily blaming a strong gut feeling on a lack of breakfast, "everybody gets them."

As the service started, my gut talked louder and louder: What are you doing? Are you nuts? Are you crazy? This isn't right!

My reason pushed back with, "only jitters."

I endured the whole procedure, which is what it felt like, a procedure. I can't even remember it. Even as I write this, I am struggling to remember the year and the date. I remember saying I do, and being fairly amused by it all, putting the ring I had bought myself on my own finger, the off-white blouse... it's all robotic and unromantic.

We didn't make a big deal to my friends and family and Steven didn't tell any of his family in Canada; yet, I felt so honored that this clever, intelligent, and good-looking man wanted to marry me.

Wasn't I lucky?

After the procedure, the four of us dined in a Turkish restaurant to celebrate the wedding. Awkwardly, I paid for Steven and I, since he had gone bust again the night before.

We headed home to our wedding night, the happiest night in the life of a newlywed, our first night together as a married couple. I strolled into the bedroom, feeling not a little amorous. Steven followed closely behind, taking off his shirt. The excitement of anticipation grew inside me, a knowing smile on my face. Sure, we had no money and our wedding was as bare-bones as could be, but what did it matter as long as we had love? We were in love, weren't we? And love, they say, is all you need.

Steven reached into the drawer for a clean shirt.

"Wait, what are you doing?" I said.

"Going to work, why?" he said, matter of fact, as though I were already being unreasonable.

"What do you mean you're going to work?" I said, the tears welling up.

"Sam, we didn't really get married today," he said. "It was the registry office. We're getting married in a few months—in Vegas, remember? So, right now, I'm going to work."

I was utterly astounded. Our wedding night was only in my mind. I didn't have any confidence for a debate with him, and he long ago mastered wordplay over me. I would never be able to win an intellectual argument with Steven, and should I get emotional, he would disregard me completely. The outcome of this contest was certain. With nothing else to say, I let him go.

I knew this was how Steven thought, so why was I surprised? If he believed something a certain way, that's the way it was. It didn't occur to him to consider that I might want it to be even a little bit special, or for him to have any sentiment or attachment; nor did he adjust his thinking when he found out I did. It had nothing to do with how he felt about me, and it had nothing to do with love. It was just the way he was: intellectual, cool, reasonable—and totally demoralizing.

That evening at home, alone, was cold and dark. The flat was damp and the smell of mold mixed with the all-pervading curry in the air. I wrapped myself up in blankets on the sofa, turned on the T.V. and started to eat everything I could find in the fridge. The phone rang a few times, friends and family calling with congratulations, but I never picked up. I didn't want anybody to know I was home by myself on my wedding night in some cold and moldy apartment. I fell into to my wedding bed and cried hard until sleep came.

All my confidence in my looks, sex appeal, and any enthusiasm for romance left me that night. I woke up in the middle of the night and there was no Steven, and I thought, He has to be joking. He'll realize when he gets to the casino and he'll come home with flowers or chocolates or something and we'll have a proper wedding night. But he didn't come home until 7 a.m., his usual time, and all he wanted to do was surf the internet and then go to bed.

After that, I slipped into an unconscious pattern of avoidance. I did everything possible to keep busy and distract myself from my marriage. I would work on Aspire during the day, Steven would play poker at night. Almost like we were on different ships once again.

I remember back when we were together on ship in Puerto Rico, when one evening at port Steven took me to a casino in San Juan. He told me to sit behind him and watch as he played. The majority of poker players are men, girlfriends and wives sit back behind them to watch— that is, if they're invited. I was enthralled at the time, it was all so cool and curious. What an exciting, glamorous life this is going to be, I thought.

Steven explained how poker is a game of strategy, not luck. It's about being smart and being able to influence people. I bought into this completely. Steven was smart, like Mensa membership smart, and therefore I believed he must also be good at playing poker.

At one point in the game, he turned around and whispered into my ear, "Sam, if I don't win this next hand, I'm going to lose $30,000."

Gosh, isn't this edgy? I thought.

Steven proceeded to lose the hand. He sat there and lost $30,000.

"Okay," he said, getting up calmly, "you need to know when to cut your losses. Let's go." As we walked out into the parking lot arm in arm, he said, "How did you feel when I lost that money?"

"Quite excited, actually," I said, "and I'm sure you'll win again, the way you play." Totally naïve to the fact that the way he played had made his opponent's mortgage payment for the next two years.

"Good," he said, "because this is my life. If you want to be with me you need to understand this is how our life is going to be. It's going to be up and down and you need to be able to deal with it. Can you?"

"Yes," I said, foolishly underestimating the nature of that roller coaster. "Of course, I can deal with it," but it was blind love talking.

Steven's attitude about risk absolutely opposed mine. He could put money on the line, walk away from huge losses, and come back the very next night to lose all over again. Yet there we still had to pay rent and our other bills, and the wild income swings we experienced only made it more stressful. Sometimes he contributed significantly to handle our expenses, but usually not.

"Are you up or down this week?" I would ask.

Sometimes he would say, "Up." Mostly he would say, "Down."

But he didn't deal with losing as easily as he put on, walking away from piles of money takes its toll on anyone. His mood was often sour and he was easily irritated. He would watch T.V. and surf the internet for days at a time. I started to deal with all this in the same way people deal with trauma.

Steven tried to establish himself while I developed Aspire, so I was the only one bringing in steady money. He was passionate about poker and I wanted success for him, of course. I did my best to be supportive, but when his confidence was shaken after a long losing streak, he would go after mine. Eventually, my friends and family detected that I wasn't in the dream relationship I portrayed. When they asked if Steven was doing well, I did what any self-loathing wife of a losing poker player would do—I lied right to their faces.

I was no quitter and I believed I could get through this situation, I could turn this failing marriage around. I could change Steven and tame the beast within. I kept plugging away, trying to make it better, wishing he would change, believing our relationship would be different and it would all work out, and that it was all only a matter of time. I was good at telling myself this story.

We get skillful at telling stories to ourselves, don't we? We stay in relationships or jobs longer than we should. We eat the wrong food, we never exercise, we tolerate abuse. The signs are all there, but we ignore them.

When someone shows you who they really are, believe them.

I remember the moment I decided to leave Steven. I had been nagging him to read over some new website copy I had written. Steven was good at many activities, but he was a great writer. I left a printout for him each night so he could read it when he arrived home in the morning. It took great effort to write this new piece and I wanted his feedback and advice. In the morning, I could hear him upstairs, clacking away on the computer. He could be grumpy in the morning, especially if he had lost money the night before, so I showered and dressed before venturing upstairs, putting extra detail on my make-up to look extra nice for him.

I walked into our home office and smiled. He looked up from reading my piece for the Aspire website and said, "You know, Sam, this is shit."

Well, good morning to you, too.

In Aspire training, we practice something called a praise sandwich. Whenever you're required to give anyone feedback, you first comment on something positive, then you remark about the areas needing improving, then you end your remarks with another positive. Steven constantly gave me the opposite of a praise sandwich—more like a shit sandwich. I tried to stay calm, but the steady stream of criticism eroded not only my self-esteem, but my patience also.

I spoke up, saying, "Steven, there's this thing we call the praise sandwich. I wonder if next time you give me some feedback on something I've written, you could do it in this way..." And I gently explained how the praise sandwich worked.

"No problem," he said. "I like your hair. Your writing is shit. Your shoes aren't bad either." Then he practically passed out laughing.

At that moment it hit home for me; I was married to a man with zero emotional intelligence. I had done all I could do, gone as far as I could go. I wanted out.

But it takes confidence to leave a relationship, and by then Steven had robbed me of all mine. I relied on those drug-like surges whenever he told me he loved me, or I looked good, or I had lost a little weight.

I looked for him constantly to say, "I love you, and it's all going to be okay. You're amazing, you're beautiful, you're gorgeous," which he had stopped doing years before, if he had ever done it at all.

Emma disliked Steven immensely, often telling me, "Leave him. You're going to be okay. You'll be fine. Come stay with us."

I couldn't hear it and I often made excuses, "You don't know him like I do. You don't see him like I do."

I had lost myself.

Where was the confident little five-year-old Sam, running off to find out what was on the other side of a great hill; the wise seven-year-old in her bedroom, unjustly punished and vowing to be good to others; the teenage Sam, ready to take on the world, or at least, Liverpool; the young woman fighting for her mother's rightful place in death; the one who had started a business from nothing. When I was that person, anything was possible. I didn't have to get my confidence from others, because true confidence—the kind that matters, the kind that gave me my strength—came from inside me.

You are whole, unique.

When I reviewed all the positive achievements in my life, I rediscovered me. Hey remember me? Here I am, I'm actually pretty confident, if you'll let me be confident. I needed to come back to myself, find my core self and listen to my supportive voice, which says: You can do this! You might not know exactly how you're going to do it, or how it's going to turn out, but you don't need to know that right now. All you need to know is that it's the right thing to do. You'll be okay!

It took me five long years with Steven to find her again.

The disease in our relationship started out small and finally became terminal. The daily gibes, the poker roller-coaster, the shit sandwiches, the broken promises (we never made it to Las Vegas for a real wedding, although Steven flew out a couple of times to play poker), the crying into my pillow every night, and the zero sex life which I attributed to my emotional eating and weight gain. Being unable to justify professional poker as a career choice, not even making a living wage, and going broke every other week helped the infection spread. It was a slow, grinding illness that occurs in far too many relationships, including mine.

Ending a marriage is always hard, but I had reached my breaking point. After five years, a thousand 'talks' going nowhere, and one vain attempt at marriage counseling, we divided our belongings. Steven left one night while I spoke at an event in central London, empowered as I spoke to a room full of male executives while my husband vacated our apartment. It was the lightest and most alive I had felt in years.

When my speaking engagement finished that night, I came home and stood in the hall with my key stuck in the front door, listening. Would he be gone? Or would he be standing there with flowers and excuses? I was harboring some guilt. Steven didn't have any money and I had supported him financially for years, would he even be okay?

When I opened the door the only residue left was one of his belts lying on the floor, dropped on his way out. I sighed, picked up the belt and sat down looking at it, astonished at my journey so far, and wondering if I could make it on my own.

I swore off men, deciding they were all the same, looked around the crappy flat and decided to move immediately. Time for a new start—again—but free and empowered, and a little nervous.

The people closest to us have the biggest influence on our confidence, our sense of self-worth and our happiness. In my view, the most important relationship you have is with your life partner. One of the most difficult lessons I've learned is if your partner doesn't make you feel beautiful, happy, and supported, it leads to an erosion of self esteem, depression or worse. These negative feelings can lead to the justification of their behavior and a belief that it is in fact our fault. This can take us into a state of paralysis and a lack of confidence in making a change coupled with a belief that we can not be without this person.

When we finally say, "I've had enough," or, "I'm leaving," or, "You need to leave," we may feel unsure. Such moments can feel scary from the pit of our stomachs to the ends of our toes, from the heaviness in our shoulders to a racing mind that screams, What are you doing? How are you going to do this? What's going to happen to you? It's all incredibly overwhelming, yes. But guess what? Life is made full by such moments— those moments when Radio Heaven, the universe, God, or whatever you call it looks down and says: "All right, you've done your bit. Took you a while, but you did well. Now I'm going to help you."

In the words of Goethe, "Be bold and mighty forces will come to your aid." Then suddenly, something happens. Help arrives. We see the good in negative situations.

For every negative, there is a positive not to be overlooked, and I'm grateful to Steven for helping me develop my business, even if it was in a negative way. When he told me: "You'll never be successful in business. You're too nice, and it's not possible to be nice and successful in business", it was a truth to him. He had never known anyone in the business world who was "nice" as well as successful. He thought ruthlessness and cunning were necessities in business, and anyone who was nice would meet a nasty end from the competition.

But I knew a truth, too. It was borne out by my professional conduct up to then. I was a good person and I liked being nice. I found people to work with who appreciated that about me, and I didn't enter into business with people who didn't think the same way. I made a conscious effort to spend more time with the people who empowered me, and less time, or no time at all, with those who did not. Staying true to my authentic self, and being nice, proved to have positive payoffs.

Steven didn't believe it was possible for a nice person to win. What he didn't realize was being nice didn't mean being soft or ineffective or weak. It meant treating people well while doing good business. It was my fundamental belief that a conscious business, with a focus on people and the planet as well as profits, will be successful in the future; and I fight for that belief every day.

Make good choices about who you spend the most time with, and find the courage inside to get out of bad relationships. It can be revealing, I have found, to reflect on the people you spend most time with in life, and to think about how they made you feel, and if they had a positive or negative effect on your life, career happiness, and success.

Is it time for you to conduct your own relationship audit, then take some bold action?

CHAPTER 10

Nutty Professor

Having a mentor who shares advice and experience, as well as advocating for you is a fundamental element to success in one's career. Yet, a LinkedIn survey of more than 1,000 working women revealed only 1 out of 5 have ever had a mentor. The women's networking organization Levo League conducted a survey of their users and found that 95% of women had never sought out a mentor. It seems as women we believe we can and should be able to "do it all".

When Steven and I parted ways, I packed up a big green suitcase and marched directly to the one person I could always count on, Emma. By now she and her boyfriend David had given birth to the first child of her generation in our family. Baby Serena was named after me (the 'S') and my mum's mother Rene. I slept on Emma's floor once again, this time safe and sound in little Serena's room. This time around, however, I was also trying to run a business.

Believe me, it was no easy feat sharing office space with baby Serena, especially when the child in question spills orange juice on your laptop, causing the hard drive and all else that was Aspire up to then, to disappear into the ether. I loved Serena then, and continue to adore my niece, but this was not one of our defining moments.

I needed somewhere to work, so I quickly found a small office to rent in the Guildhall, an impressive building in the heart of the City that had been used as a town hall for several hundred years. I would never have thought I could afford an office with such a prestigious address, but knowing that we were coming out of a recession, and that tenants were hard to come by, I offered £400 a month for a spacious traditional room overlooking the open Guildhall Yard. They accepted and I never looked back.

The City of London is a traditional place, filled with wealthy banks and law firms going back hundreds of years, and buildings standing since the Great Fire of 1666. It is a vibrant, fast paced area, but the culture is a male-dominated one. There are few women. Asking for help can be perceived as a sign of weakness.

Emma and I had finally repaired the relationship with our dad after so many years, and when he attended my Master's graduation ceremony, I discovered he hadn't diverted one degree (no pun intended) from his hopes for me. "Now you've done a Masters," he said, "time for a Ph.D., eh Sam?"

But I needed some help understanding the issues of women in leadership positions and particularly the women working in London in those typically male-dominated industries like banking, law, and accountancy. Since I had completed my Master's and Coach Training program, I thought the timing could be right for doing a Ph.D.

I checked myself and my motives to make sure I wasn't doing it to prove something to my dad. I weighed how it would give me more credibility and a way to research and understand women's needs for today—discovering what progress had truly been made, and uncovering what lay ahead. It would help me design Aspire programs and events specifically for the women I wanted to work with.

I must admit, I liked the sound of Dr. Collins. Who would ever imagine I could achieve something like that?

As I thought about the City of London, I thought, where better to grow my business and do a Ph.D.? If I can crack it here, I can crack it anywhere. People will tell you to start easy and work your way up. I'm the opposite. I think if you start where it's hardest, it gets easier as you go.

I researched universities in the city and found out there was a Business School in the London Guildhall University, close to my office. If I wanted to do a Ph.D., I needed a professor who would help me, mentor me, be my supervisor, and also want to take on my topic, so I embarked on a quest to find the best female professor, believing a woman would understand my needs best, but there wasn't one.

When I heard about a male professor doing interesting work on human resource development that touched on the subjects of women and work, I was intrigued. His name was Professor John Walton.

I plucked up the courage, found his phone number, and arranged a time to meet him. Getting the appointment wasn't easy, as he didn't return missed calls. But I kept calling, leaving messages, or sometimes letting the phone ring and ring. One day, he answered the phone himself and abruptly told me to come to his office the next day. I wasn't confident in my preparation in the least, but figured I could introduce myself and assess whether I would like him to be my supervisor.

Finding his office within the maze of London Guildhall University proved to be my first challenge. I found Professor Walton in a closet-size room at the back of one of the many buildings, one of the many additions put in over hundreds of years—down a long corridor, turn right, up and then down stairs, and around the corner.

The next challenge was finding the professor himself, hidden behind piles of papers and lots of odd antiques strewn all over the small room. When I saw him, the first person I thought of was Dr. Emmet Brown from Back to the Future, dressed in a wrinkled suit with his tie slightly off center. His greying hair was a little wild and I couldn't see his face as he hunched over the disarray of papers on his desk.

I bounced into his office the first time, all smiles, with a singsong, "Hello!"

"And you are? Why are you here?" he said, not looking up. I don't think he even remembered we scheduled a meeting.

"I'm Sam Collins. I want to do a Ph.D. on women and work," I said. "I've been reading all these magazines and newspaper articles saying there are only ten to fifteen percent of women on boards of directors. I think it's really low and I want to investigate. I've also started a company called Asp..." I stopped talking because he hadn't looked up at me still. Was he deaf?

He looked at me sternly, tilting back in his seat. "Magazines and newspapers," he said, "this is an academic institution, my dear. May I suggest you go away for six months and read every academic journal you can find on this issue of yours? If you're still interested at that point, come back to me. Now you can leave."

Some mentor.

"Okay," I said quietly, and left. What else could I do? The professor had put me firmly in my place, and I realized the naïveté of reading the Financial Times for insights on my topic—it wasn't going to get me a Ph.D.

Who was I to think I could do a Ph.D., anyway?

But the professor made an impression, and I huddled in the university library whenever I could to read every academic study published on women and leadership. Some of the time, I couldn't even understand the title and there were words I didn't even know existed. Sometimes, as I read at night after a day of working at Aspire, I fell asleep in the library over my papers.

Over time though, the reading helped and I started to get a bigger picture of the issues at play. I read everything I could find about the lack of women at board level and the plethora of reasons why. I also found it frustrating, because everything I read, more or less, focused on why there aren't many women in senior positions. I read little offering any solutions as to what should be done, or what the future held for women in the workplace.

I returned to John's office almost six months later to the day—unannounced. I hung around outside his office for a while, listening for signs of life and plucking up the courage to go in. When I finally knocked, a polite "Come in!" reverberated from the pile of papers on the desk.

He didn't remember me at first. He told me later, he tells every potential doctorate student to go off for six months and come back, and I was the first person in a long while to actually do so, and definitely the first woman.

John listened to me and then explained that my frustration with the literature was good. He explained Ph.D.s born out of frustration, born from a gap in the literature. He suggested a study of the future, rather than the past, and that discussing a What, rather than a Why, would be more valuable. He seemed excited by the topic and knew instinctively I would need a lot of help and support to achieve a Ph.D. We started to formulate my proposal.

I embarked on my study: "The Future World of Work for Women Leaders".

John was my nutty professor, my mentor, and the supervisor for my Ph.D. over the next seven years as I balanced a part time doctorate with building Aspire. I found earning a Ph.D. was extremely hard. Studying at this level hurt my head and I had so little time. I wanted to give up regularly and when I did, I asked for help from John. We met on an irregular basis, sometimes once a month or once a week, sometimes once every couple of months, depending on where I was with my research.

I am so grateful to John for his never-ending support. He pushed the idea for me to do a more creative Ph.D. than I thought possible; one looking to the future world of work for women as leaders. He made it possible for me to do this using my coaching visioning techniques, storytelling, and creative writing techniques and we had fun finding methodologies that suited our approach. We duplicated how futurists work and used many academic ideas behind futurism. I'm incredibly grateful to John for this in particular, because it made my Ph.D. exactly what I wanted to write. I wanted to focus on what could be, what the future might look like for women, and not what was already happening. He was brilliant at letting me be me as much as possible within the confines of the doctorate rules.

One day in a café at the train station at Harrow on the Hill, I met with John and he showed me Adair's Model of Management, which is made up of three concentric circles: one is task, one is team, and one is individual. A good manager focuses on meeting the needs of all three in balance. The task needs attention, the team needs attention, and each person on the team needs attention.

"The trouble with you, Sam," John said, "is you're too task-focused." He was right, of course. "What we are going to do, even though I know you find it very frustrating, is we're going to talk about my antiques for at least ten minutes every time you come in, because that's something important to me as an individual, and something you need to learn."

So from then on, we spent the first ten minutes of our sessions talking about his acquisitions around his office, from Asia to eBay. I found it extremely boring at first, but he helped me understand why we can't always focus on what needs to be done without focusing on the individuals involved in doing it. It was critical to be empathetic to individual dreams and inspirations, as well as the collective aspirations of the team. I thank John dearly for this knowledge.

Midway through the program he told me, "You're doing really well considering you're not an academic."

"What's that supposed to mean?" I said.

"Well, you're not an academic, Sam. You are a practitioner. Your topic is well, flaky."

Excuse me?

"I chose to let you do this the way you wanted to do it, because otherwise I think you would have given up."

It was true. If John asked me do this in a traditional academic way, I wouldn't have lasted a year. Because he let me do it in a more creative way, though I still backed up my methodologies academically, it made everything so much more exciting.

I like to think it made it more exciting for him, too.

John taught me that you couldn't force people into going down a certain road and expect them to be successful. Sometimes you have to have the courage to let people go down their own road. Believe me, it does take courage and confidence to do this; a weak or meek person would rely on rigid rules and procedures to guide them rather than taking the risk of trying something new and unconventional.

My philosophy was always to do only what I was good at and enjoyed. I wasn't particularly good at academic writing, and I didn't enjoy it, so, while it was contrary to my nature, it was important to me to accept the challenge of going outside my normal comfort zone, because I would be producing something to outlast me.

Sometimes we need to make careful choices. Just because we're not good at something, or we don't enjoy it, doesn't necessarily mean we shouldn't do it, and you can learn a new way or notice new options along the way. I didn't know when I embarked on doing the Ph.D. with John there would be a creative way of writing it until I actually started writing it.

Earning my Ph.D. wasn't easy. After seven years and a 100,000-word thesis, I attended my final panel interview with several professors in and outside of the university to defend my thesis. This event is a bit like being in court—they ask, you defend. It takes a lot of preparation to make this defense. John helped me prepare extensively in advance and chose the outside supervisor carefully, advocating my work and me beforehand. He was my sponsor, and because his reputation was impeccable, so was mine.

But I couldn't even pronounce some of the words in my thesis, "The epistemology was a phenomenological approach." I couldn't say it for days. I can still hardly say the word phenomenology, and, first time around, they didn't let me pass.

After a rewrite of the final section, they confirmed me. A bloody fantastic day. Dr. Sam Collins, for now and forever. Earning a Ph.D. has opened many doors for me and given me a level of confidence and credibility I never realized was possible. I will never forget the moment I changed my email signature to Dr. Samantha Collins—incredible.

I finished the journey with a newfound determination and respect for myself, and a true appreciation for my mentor and sponsor, Professor John Walton. You, too, should experience the power and importance of finding good mentors and sponsors. Get clear on what you want from them, as well as working out who might actually fit the bill, and then be proactive about 'claiming' them.

It is good and necessary to ask for help. It is not a sign of weakness, but a sign of strength and intelligence. Having a mentor is fundamental to maintaining motivation and being opened up to new ideas. As women in a male-oriented world, we need as many mentors as we can find, and it is our responsibility to mentor others once we succeed.

CHAPTER 11

The Ordeal

According to Joseph Campbell's The Hero's Journey, the heroine experiences what is called an ordeal. Near the middle of the story, she enters into battle, facing her greatest fears, demons, or even death itself; but from that moment of death springs new life and a stronger character. In the same way, we can experience incredibly difficult times and phases in our lives. These times, trying as they may be, effectively build living confidence and active self-belief.

After Steven and I parted ways, and a few weeks on Emma's floor, I found a lovely little cottage to rent: a 15th century coach-house on a corner of a nice street in Harrow-on-the-Hill, in Northwest London, nearby to Emma. I was born in Harrow-on-the-Hill and lived there as a baby. It was comforting to find a place near my roots, and even better to be all on my own. I also vowed not to date anyone for at least a year, because I wanted to discover whether I could survive completely on my own, without a man, spending time by myself, and learning to enjoy my own company. I needed to regain my confidence and find me again.

It was incredibly hard spending nights alone—I worked late, ate Marks & Spencer TV-dinners, and drank wine—night after night by myself. Until eventually I realized I wasn't all by myself, not exactly.

The little cottage sat on the edge of what used to be an old manor house estate. A long time ago it served as the gatekeeper's house. I later discovered there was only a single gatekeeper who ever lived there through its heyday. I sensed a distinctly lonely feeling inside the cottage, and thought it was all from me. You could certainly argue that I felt lonely because of my situation, but I had spent time on my own before, so it was unfamiliar. But the emotions inside the house weren't the only thing unfamiliar.

After about a year I began having unusual physical symptoms. A cancer scan revealed abnormal cervical cancer cells, and I needed immediate and serious medical attention to eliminate them. I felt like my life was going from bad to worse and hated being unwell. I despaired about the cancer developing and found myself questioning whether I could survive on my own. I had to have a number of treatments, and after one of the most painful my doctor unceremoniously told me I would probably have trouble being pregnant and carrying a baby to term. Babies were the last thing on my mind as I trudged home from that treatment and crawled into bed.

That night, as I was tossing and turning in bed and half asleep, I heard quiet music coming from somewhere—it sounded like violin music. It scared me. It was creepy and I rose from my bed and looked out of the window expecting to see some weird musician on the street, but there was nothing. I tiptoed down the stairs, turning the lights on in my bedroom first, then the hall. When I flicked on the lamp downstairs, the music stopped. I sighed, turned off the lights in reverse order and traipsed back upstairs.

As soon as I lay down the music started up again.

I looked out of the windows again to check whether someone was trying to give me a midnight serenade—nope. Again I walked downstairs doing the light routine. The music stopped.

I suddenly felt calm and I felt a presence in the room. A comforting presence. I was aware somehow that I was not alone in this old house. I am not a believer in ghosts and ghouls and am terrified at the thought. This was not like this. I had a feeling that I was being soothed by the music. There was an energy in the house that was there to try to protect me and I liked it. I stood in the lounge, put my hands firmly on my hips and said aloud, "Thank you. I hear you, but I do need to get some sleep now please." I returned upstairs. The music stopped but the soothing feeling stayed.

A friend of mine who is acutely sensitive to afterlife energies told me, yes, there was the presence of a man who had lived there a very long time. He used to be the gatekeeper and it was his job to protect and serve. Initially I freaked out, but I acclimated to the idea, learning to live with the silent energy around me. It soon became normal and a source of company.

Until living in the cottage became weirder.

One Saturday, about 1 a.m., I was upstairs in my bedroom sleeping when someone started banging on the door—not knocking, but frantically pounding the door off its hinges. This time it was no ghost, this time it was a very real, very angry man.

"Let me in," he screamed, "I'm coming in!"

My heart started pounding, the phone was downstairs and I needed to get to it before he broke the door down. I crept downstairs slowly, trying not to make noise, but I panicked and shouted as authoritatively as I could muster, "Go away, please. I'm calling the police!" I was frightened out of my wits. "You're at the wrong house, go away."

"No, I'm not!" He kept screaming, "I know James is in there. I'm coming around the back."

Terrified, I ran to the phone and dialed the police. A woman operator answered and I whispered to her as I hid on the stairs, out of sight of the door, "Please, someone is trying to break into my house. I need help!"

Meanwhile, I tried to peek out of the back windows. There he was, by the kitchen door now, brandishing a huge knife. You have to be kidding me; I have a knife-wielding psychopath at my door?

"I'm going to kill you! I'm going to kill you both," he screamed.

I've never, ever been so scared. The blood drained out of me as this lunatic rattled the door—the back kitchen door like so many other back kitchen doors, not nearly as sturdy as the front door.

I cried and screamed into the phone, "You need to get here now. He's breaking in!"

"There's a car there now," the operator said, "but they can't find your house."

That's because the cottage didn't have a house number, only the name.

"I'm going to need you to hang up now," the operator said.

"What? Why? What are you talking about?"

"The policemen in the car are going to call you directly so they can find you," she said, "it's going to be okay."

I hung up. I don't know how long it was before the police car called, seconds maybe, but it felt like ages. They finally came around the back and wrestled the crazed man to the ground. He was drunk and on drugs, and kept repeating his boyfriend's name, insisting we were in my house together. He was handcuffed and driven away.

After that, I was pretty well driven away myself. I immediately jumped in my car and drove to Emma's house. She said I was white. We might be English, but she had never before seen me such a pale shade.

I stayed away from the cottage for a week. When I did go back, my friend Julia came along and stayed a few days. Thank you to Julia for always being there for me wherever I have lived, and whenever I've needed you!

I sensed a weird heaviness in the house, as if it had built up so much bad energy it was now attracting bad energy in from outside. It affected me when I was in a bad state and, despite the soothing energy, nothing much good came of living there.

Environment is important. As much as we need to trust our gut about people, we ought to be conscious of the same when it comes to our environment. Some houses, offices, and other places are better to avoid. Places can hold energy, good or bad, and it can rub off on you—this is a powerful truth and not to be treated lightly.

In the end, I survived being alone and dealing with my demons in the haunted cottage for an entire year. I faced ghosts both inside and outside. I faced a cancer scare and a crazed man, overcoming each of them by myself.

And not only was I still alive, I was good. Everything was good. I hadn't relied on anybody, and I survived my ordeal. The experience changed me. Was it easy? No. Would I do it alone again? Not unless I had to. But having that extended period of time between relationships, taking a break to discover the real me and how I might cope with life on my own was incredibly valuable. My confidence returned slowly, and I was able to start to wonder what my "dream life" could be on the other side of the ordeal. I felt more prepared and ready for whatever, or whoever, was coming into my life next.

Let me encourage you now to face your fears, and be confident you can make it independently at least part of the way. There is huge strength and confidence in looking your darkest fears in the face. You'll live to tell your tale!

CHAPTER 12

Desperately

"So, did you work on it?"

"Yes."

"How was it?"

"I really enjoyed creating it," I said. "It was great, especially after the second glass of wine!" Gosia laughed and I continued, "I taped it on the ceiling above my bed so I can look at it every day, first thing in the morning."

"I've never heard of that before," she said, "great idea!"

I thought for a second and said, "The trouble is, Gosia, it's not working."

"What do you mean by not working?"

"I mean, it's been a month and nothing has changed."

"Well, sometimes you have to be patient, Sam."

It was October 2006 and I had come down from an extremely busy few years. Aspire was now doing great, my divorce from Steven was finalized, and I had moved out of the haunted cottage and bought my first home (an un-haunted Victorian townhouse in the village of Rickmansworth in Hertfordshire).

I did want to sort out a few areas of my life—namely, finding the man of my dreams—but had no clue about how to make that happen. So in the spirit of practicing what I preach, I hired a coach.

For our first session, Gosia gave me this assignment: Create a vision board. In case you are unfamiliar:

Vision Board Ingredients

1 large, blank piece of flip chart paper or poster board

Pair of scissors

Glue stick

Magazines

Magazines

More magazines

Instructions: Flip through the magazines and rip out any pictures, words, colors, or textures resonating with you, or capturing an element of your ideal life. We're talking total and absolute perfection here. What you want to do, how much income you want, who you want to become, where you want to live, what relationships you want to develop; anything that would make you happy, successful, and feeling beautiful should be glued to your board.

One more thing: it's critically important to be instinctive in your selection of images—in other words, send your brain on temporary vacation! You need to set yourself a fairly short time limit for this in order to minimize the temptation to drift off into reading all those fascinating articles you're flicking through.

And once the glue dries it all comes true.

Yeah, right!

But Gosia came highly recommended. Plus, after two glasses of wine to help quiet that pesky little voice a few decibels, I started enjoying the process of the vision board. I found it unexpectedly clarifying and helpful to discover what I really wanted from life—a valuable exercise in and of itself.

Little did I know...

I remember coming across the picture of my ideal man: ruggedly handsome, deep eyes, graying hair, a real Sean Connery type. He carried a little boy on his shoulders, and the caption read: Playful yet serious.

"Wow! If only I could find a man like that." And yes, I talked out loud the whole time I worked on this crazy thing. I cut out the picture and glued it down alongside some others of California. After finishing the vision board and sticking it on the ceiling above my bed, (hoping it wouldn't fall on me during the night) I fell asleep and dreamed of living in California with my Sean Connery look-alike, making beautiful babies.

I carried on for about a month until this conversation with Gosia. She advised me not to merely view it on the wall, but feel it. So every day, at night and each morning, I would look at my vision board and try to feel it. This made for some pleasant nights, and rather enticing daydreams.

"But there must be something else I can do to get this thing going."

"What actions do you think you could you take?"

"You never told me it was action-oriented," I said, "if it's action oriented, that's my thing. I'm Action Girl. I thought I had to feel it."

"No, you still have to do something."

"Okay, I can take action," I said. "What action should I take?"

"What action do you think you should take?" How annoying is it when coaches throw your question right back at you? I had no idea. Since I'm paying her the big bucks shouldn't she tell me?

Sometimes we need a little pushback.

"In other words," Gosia said, "what is your gut telling you to do?"

"I think my gut is telling me that my dream man is not in London. He's not even in England. I have all these pictures of California on my vision board. Maybe he's in California?"

#

The next day, I received an e-mail inviting me to the annual International Coach Federation industry conference. Well, that's interesting. Was it in California? No. It was in St. Louis, Missouri— closer to California than me at the moment. At least the conference looked interesting, so if nothing else it could be refreshing to travel to a different environment and meet a few new people and learn something useful about coaching. My gut told me it would be a good idea to get out of England and do something different.

Still, it was not an easy decision, and no small feat for me to take a week out of my business to fly to America. And for what, said the pesky little voice, to attend a conference that isn't any different from the ones in England? I struggled over going to this conference, but I buried that voice and took the plunge. After all, I loved to travel, and any trip combining travel and work has some merit! Besides, was there power in this vision board thing, or would it turn out to be nothing more than a poster full of pretty little pictures?

"Let's find out," I said, "St. Louis, Missouri—first stop to taking action!"

Two weeks and one long flight later, I sat on the edge of a bed in a hotel room, hungry and thirsty with a throbbing sciatica pain in my right leg. There was a mixer about to start downstairs for other coaches who had been through the same training program as me. I planned to say a quick hello to the few people I knew, grab a bite, and come back upstairs to my room for a good night's sleep.

I made my way downstairs, still wearing my clothes from the plane: ripped jeans, t-shirt, ill-fitting pink cardigan, jacket, and a little leftover makeup applied before I boarded the flight. It would do and this would take a half-hour, tops. After that: Sleep, here I come!

There was a great spread of food downstairs and I was starving. I set my jacket down, piled up my plate, and walked over to grab a glass (or two) of Cabernet. I stuck a cracker in my mouth and eyeballed the situation to calculate how I could carry my plate, my jacket, and two glasses of wine back up to my room without anyone noticing me. Oh, I'll socialize tomorrow, I thought.

When I looked up, however, there was a man walking towards me. I looked down at my plate for balance and then back up and... Is he? Why is he looking at me? Then suddenly—and believe me, I know how this sounds—like a Mills & Boon film (British for Harlequin Romance) the world around me literally dissolved and all I could see was this divinely handsome man, walking toward me...

In. Slow. Motion.

And then it hit me: Holy shit! It's the Sean Connery from my vision board! I nearly choked on my cracker.

His lips moved like he was talking. He was saying something, looking into my eyes and talking and smiling. What is he saying? I didn't speak. I couldn't speak or hear anything at all. He looked so exactly like the picture of the man from my vision board (without a little boy on his shoulders, of course).

What is this—a joke? If I blink will he evaporate? Is my jet lag so bad I'm now hallucinating?

He was well dressed, with salt and pepper graying hair (check), looking like Sean Connery (check, check), and did I happen to mention more handsome than anyone I'd ever seen (check, check, check). And those eyes. Whew! I was so drawn into his eyes.

"Can I help you with that?" He repeated, thinking I hadn't heard. True. I hadn't.

Two sentences reverberated in my mind: Please don't be married. Please don't be gay. I sneakily checked for a wedding ring. He wasn't wearing one (check, check, check, check).

"Oh, yes," I said, thinking I should say something—or blurt something, as the case may be. Oh! Please don't be married. Please don't be gay. I kept thinking.

"Maybe I'll have some wine, too," he said, still smiling.

I think I smiled. I don't know. I'm not sure what my face was up to. What is wrong with you, Sam? I thought. He kept talking, I kept looking. I still couldn't hear well. Then the most horrifying thought popped into my mind: Oh God, I'm not wearing any makeup, he's going to think I'm a right pig with this great big pile of food on my plate! Not only that, I was still wearing my clothes from the plane. Shabby? Yes. Chic? Hardly. I probably smelled bad, too. He must think I'm crashing the event to steal something to eat. This made me laugh, out loud!

And now he thinks I'm crazy.

I was face to face with a hybrid of Sean Connery and Harrison Ford, both on an incredibly good day, with piercing green-grey eyes, and dressed smartly in black jeans and a dark blue jacket. What is that, velvet? Yes, please.

"You're English," he said, gathering a clue from my single utterance. "I'm English, too."

His accent was too American. Yeah, sure, I thought, probably thinks it's a great pick-up line, even though the last of his family to set foot on the British Isles was in 1775. But I believe in being nice, so I played along. "Oh, you're English?" I said, "Where from?"

"I'm from Manchester," he said, still sounding very American.

"Oh?" I said looking cynical.

"Aye, lass, I'm from Manchester," he said, in that broad northern accent that gives me goose flesh.

I melted. "You are indeed from Manchester," I said, instantly and totally smitten with this man from the North of England, who then told me he now lived in California.

Hello, and thank you, Radio Heaven!

But instead of saying the next thing that raced into my head, which was, "Did you know I did a vision board with you on it and I'm going marry you?" I casually dipped a carrot stick into some dressing and took a bite.

"Should we go and sit down somewhere?" He said.

"That would be lovely."

I looked around for my jacket but I couldn't find it anywhere. At that moment, though, I didn't care if I never wore it again. As for my cell phone... Oh hell, I can always get a new phone. I don't have any other way to describe my attraction to him other than instantaneous and electrifying.

We drank some wine together and then he ordered two Grand Marnier on the rocks, which I had never tried before. We sat at the bar hour after hour filling the other one in on what had happened in our lives up to then, as if we had already known each other many years, and finally had the chance to catch up.

His name was Robert Silverstone. He was nineteen years older than me and he was originally from Manchester, but now lived in California. (I know, right?) He had come out to California in his twenties after making a success of, and subsequently selling, his family business in the U.K.; a former executive of a multi-million pound business, an entrepreneur, owning his own business for several years, which he had also sold, and he was now working from home, mentoring and coaching other would-be business owners. He was also remarkably Zen, having studied Buddhism and even once considered becoming a monk, although I was glad he didn't follow that particular career path. He paid great attention to every detail of what I said, and I was equally as interested in his musings.

It was pure and utter bliss.

Until he asked, "So, do you want to have children someday?"

"Desperately!" I blurted uncontrollably.

O. M. G. The words no sooner left my desperate lips, when a wave of desperate embarrassment swept over me. Where the hell did that come from? I wanted to run far away and never come back. I paused, smiled, looked at him with my professional face, and in my professional voice said, "Would you excuse me a moment, please?"

I walked to the bathroom, scolding myself all the way to the mirror. Once safely behind closed doors, I put my hands down flat on the counter, leaned forward, looked at myself in the mirror and said, "What the hell is wrong with you? Do you think you can go back out there now after that? Do you think he's even going to be there? It would serve you right if you walked out there now and he had disappeared thinking he'd met Fatal Attraction Bunny Boiler Part Two."

There was the little voice again. It had served me to ignore it in the past, but now it was actually coming out from my own mouth—would this be the day it was proved right? I dreaded finding out. I really wanted Robert to still be at the bar when I came back out. I sucked up my courage, put a smile on my face and opened the bathroom door.

He hadn't moved, and remained good-looking as ever. He told me long after, at the point I said desperately, he actually thought to himself, "My God, I am going to have children with this woman!" A colossal notion to Robert, then 53-years old.

We spent another several pleasant hours getting to know each other. Close to midnight he asked if he could walk me to the elevator. I was a little tipsy at this point and remembered I didn't have my jacket or phone. We started to hunt for it, but it was nowhere to be found. Robert, however, stayed calm.

"I know we'll find your jacket," he said.

Sure enough we did, someone had taken it to another room. I discovered a lot about Robert that day, but most importantly, if he says he's going to do something, he does it; and he is a model-perfect gentleman as he's doing it. We had a conference starting in the morning, so I wasn't too concerned I would never see him again.

"Goodnight, it was very nice meeting you," he said. He took my hand and shook it.

"Yes. See you in the morning," I said.

I half-floated back to my room mulling over his handshake. Didn't he fancy me as much as I guessed? Still, before falling asleep, the fantasies I was used to envisioning with a mystery man, now had a name and a voice and lived near the beach in California. We would get married with nice rings this time, we would have wonderful children, we would be so happy and in love. I would bring Aspire to America.

How was all this supposed to work?

The next morning I crawled out of bed early, drank a strong coffee, and dressed. I ran downstairs to check email on my laptop because I couldn't get internet reception in my room, and then ran back up to get finish getting ready for the day and then returned for breakfast. During the short time I was out, unbeknownst to me, Robert called my room to ask if I wanted to join him for breakfast and I had missed it. Try, try again!

There were over a thousand people at this conference, the breakfast dining room was filled to the hilt. I found a place to sit, and I looked about to find Robert, spotting him only a few tables away, but his table was full too.

Damn!

When I noticed someone get up and leave his table, that voice started in again. Should I go over and talk to him? Maybe he doesn't like me because he didn't actually say he liked me. We didn't even have a goodnight kiss. In the end I was still a woman of action, so I plowed right on.

I walked over to Robert and smiled saying, "Good morning, how are you?"

"Great! Hi! How are you?" he said in his Manchester-American accent. "Did you have a nice breakfast? Are you going into the conference now?"

"Yes, would you like to join me?"

"Of course!" Now that's more like it!

We talked a bit as we walked together. As we found our seats in the conference room, they were playing Imagine by John Lennon:

Imagine there's no heaven,

It's easy if you try

No hell below us

Above us only sky

"This was my mum's favorite song," I told Robert.

"It's my favorite song, too," he said.

Radio Heaven.

The song made me think about Mum and how I missed her! She'd like Robert, I thought, and she'd probably try and nab him for herself! I laughed to myself. I managed to sneak a peek at Robert and I was amazed to see him crying. It turned out the song reminded him of his father. I was moved and surprised to find he was actually crying, that this strong and masculine man wasn't ashamed to cry. If I had fallen in love with the idea of Robert the night before, I fell in love with Robert for real in that moment.

The session finished, and we continued to be polite to each other. There were lots of breakout workshops, so I proceeded off to one, and he walked off to another. Since the conference was two days long, I figured we had plenty of time to get to know each other more. The funny thing was, during the day, even though there were multiple workshops to attend, we kept bumping into each other. I would go into a workshop and find him on the other side of the room nearly every time. We kept being thrown together, and dancing around each other, polite and proper all the way.

Towards the end of the second day I bumped into him again. There was a big event in the evening, a ball, and I was looking forward to seeing him there.

"It was so nice meeting you," I said to him.

"Me, too," he said. "It was nice to meet you. Maybe I could do some workshops or something in England? We can connect up!"

The last thing I want to do with you is a workshop, I wanted to say. Instead I said, "Well, I hope to see you at tonight's ball."

"Oh!" he said, "I'm actually not going to be able to make it, I'm heading back to L.A. tonight."

Devastation. The wind came right out of my sails. My master plan wasn't going to work, but I smiled politely and said, "Well, it was really very nice to meet you."

"Me, too," his answer was too casual for me.

"No, no." I said aloud. I looked him in the eyes, silently sending out the thought; I thought we had more going on here. "I really enjoyed meeting you," I said with a knowing stare, get it?

He got it.

"Oh, I see! Yes, well, let's sit down and talk. A cab is coming for me in half an hour, we have a little time."

In my head, I was a little panicked—one last half-hour with Robert to make an indelible impression before he disappeared from my life for who knew how long. Maybe forever. We sat and talked. I should say: we sat, he talked, I flirted. He seemed to be playing along, he must have felt the same connection that was blossoming inside me.

His taxi arrived.

"You should come out to California and see me."

"Okay," I said.

"Then I'll call you tomorrow." He smiled and looked at me for a long time, then reached out to give me a hug. He climbed into the cab with his colleague Lisa, and they drove off. Robert is fond of telling me that in the cab on their way to the airport, Lisa said, "Were you flirting with that girl?"

"No, my dear," he replied, "that wasn't flirting, that was the real thing."

Good to his word, Robert called me the next day. Almost the first thing he said after hello was, "If we're going to have something here, you need to know I've been married before. I hope you can accept that."

"Well," I said, "I've been married before, too. So, I hope you can accept that."

And that was the start of Rob-Sam.

Without a clear and inspiring vision of exactly what you want, you will never reach it or have it. Your vision board will astonish you because it works. I urge you to have fun making one, and allow yourself for once to dream big about your ideal life, work and world. What would you love to be involved with? What would you love to achieve in the next couple of years if there were no obstacles at all? Who would you like to become?

Please give yourself this gift!

And don't forget to then take a bold action, leaps or baby-steps, it doesn't matter. If I hadn't tuned in to the email message I received, I guess I never would have gone to the conference and, who knows, might still be gazing at a peeling vision board on my ceiling every night dreaming of Robert Silverstone, instead of living with him and our beautiful children.

CHAPTER 13

California Dreamin'

Julia, my good friend, hardly ever shouts, and she had never shouted at me before.

"You're what?" she said. "You met this guy for a couple of hours, you've talked on the phone, and now you're in Heathrow about to board a flight going to Los Angeles? Are you crazy?"

"Yes, I probably am a little bit," I said, more calm than she; a little irritated she didn't trust me enough to buy in, even a little. "I have such a good feeling about him. I don't know, I can't really explain it."

"Sam, he's practically a stranger. He could be a mad axe-murderer!"

"Come on, really?" I said, "What do I really have to lose? The absolute worst-case scenario is I'll have a quick holiday in California. It's not so bad."

"Please, be careful," she said, resigned. "Text me when you get there."

Julia is a six-foot blond powerhouse from Kansas City, Missouri, who made a huge success of herself as an entrepreneur, growing a multi-million pound business from the ground up in London. She is a great friend, and truly believed she had my best interests at heart. Normally she is the risk taker, but now that I was taking a risk, she wanted to make sure I was thinking it through.

Sometimes those closest to us can prevent us from answering our true calling. Most of the time they act out of their own fear and a sense of safety. They don't want us taking risks they wouldn't take, or doing anything to result in our getting hurt in ways they wouldn't want to be hurt, either physically or emotionally. "Better safe than sorry" is an old cliché for a reason; a great many people live their lives firmly planted in that lifeless philosophy.

But I knew.

I knew myself. I knew I felt something strong with Robert and I would regret it for the rest of my life if I didn't follow through. Would his bright light die out for me after spending more than two continuous days in the same city? Unless I jumped in, how would I know?

And what if it was magical? What if everything on my vision board came to fruition the way it was meant to be? Wouldn't I be cheating myself out of the life I wanted by letting doubts take over my thinking?

Not to say I wasn't nervous. Of course I was. It was a leap of faith to travel halfway across the world, a huge leap of faith, and I took the step along with the help of a couple of vodka tonics on the plane to steady the nerves. I also checked and rechecked my face in the mirror several dozen times to confirm my makeup was perfect before landing at LAX.

Robert waited for me at the airport gate wearing something he calls his Topanga jacket. It's sort of brown and red with lots of different colors and patterns in it, and he certainly stood out in the crowded terminal. I walked out, trying not to look like I had just stepped off a transatlantic flight, or that I was exceptionally nervous. He saw me first and strode over. This time he wasn't so genteel—he grabbed me and pushed me up against a wall and gave me a fantastic kiss.

Whew. I completely melted. Yeah, right decision.

On the drive to back his house Robert asked, "Are you into Christmas?"

"Yes, I love Christmas."

"Do you want to go buy a Christmas tree?"

On December 11, 2006 we bought our first Christmas tree, tied it on the roof of the car and brought it home. Robert didn't have any decorations because he is Jewish, so he had never celebrated Christmas before, but his desire to experience everything and explore new ideas with me was so attractive! We ran back out again to buy all the decorations. I love decorating Christmas trees, and it reminds me of my mum and happy times at home, so it was a wonderful time picking out the ornaments and then arranging them. When I was done, we ceremoniously turned on the Christmas lights together.

My vision board was spot on: I glued down pictures of sunny California, and here I was. I glued down pictures of this playful yet serious guy, and here he was. We bought a Christmas tree together, decorated it together, and we were laughing and having a wonderful time in balmy 79 degree weather in December. I was living the dream. It was perfect.

And it totally freaked me out.

About ten days into our three-week visit, I sat in Robert's living room on the floor after a lovely morning. He had made me a delicious cup of coffee and my empty mug sat in front of me. He walked past, picking up the cup to take it into the kitchen. For my life I could not explain why, but it annoyed me.

"I can pick up my own coffee cup," I said, curtly.

"Wow," he said, "you've not been cared for in a long time."

"What do you mean?" I reacted, "I can take care of myself. I'm independent. I don't need a man looking after me." I stood up and looked him in the eye. "I have to go. I have to go back to England. I'm sorry."

"Okay," Robert said.

"Okay."

This tension was building inside me from the very beginning. Robert perceived the problem right away—I wasn't okay with being cared for, or comfortable with affection and attention. Steven had burned me so badly and mistreated me so often, I thought my recovery meant learning to spend time on my own. I'd grown accustomed to being completely independent. I liked not needing anything from anyone. It was safer. So when Robert Silverstone came along, giving me everything I could have possibly asked for, everything I could have possibly wanted, I couldn't take it. I was afraid. I ran.

"You need to do what you need to do," Robert said simply. He didn't fight with me. He didn't like the idea, but he didn't get upset or beg me to stay. He let me pack my belongings and drove me back to the airport. I apologized for my outburst and told him I was sorry that it didn't work out, and we said goodbye.

Vision boards are a load of crap!

I couldn't sleep on the overnight flight back to London. I stared out the window, kicking myself over my stupidity. Could I actually have it all? Do dreams really come true? What was I thinking when I walked away, leaving him in California?

It was Christmas Eve and bitterly cold when I arrived back home in Rickmansworth, back to the safety of my little village. I slid around to the side door of my Victorian town house. The door stuck, and when I pushed it in I launched indoors, falling into the stairs and hurting my knee. "Serves you right," I said.

Shoving my bags into the tiny living room, I turned on the heating, flopped down at the bottom of the steep stairway and dialed Robert's number on my phone.

He answered, "Hi."

"Robert, I've made a big mistake."

Even though it was a phone line, I could hear the smile coming up on his face. "Yes, you have," he said. "Would you like me to come over?"

"What do you mean?" I said, "Here? England?"

"Yes. If you want me to come over, I will."

"Well, that would be... that would be really great," I said.

No I told you so, no arguments, he was plain and to the point. That's Robert—and masculinity at its best.

He boarded a plane on Christmas day and arrived the day after. We proceeded to have a fantastic time. On New Year's Eve, after a few drinks at the Coach and Horses pub, a visit to the shop to buy a bottle of Grand Marnier (for old time's sake), and some takeaway Indian food, we drove back to the house and Robert said, "We're going to do a releasing ceremony tonight."

"A what?"

"We're going to release negative experiences, then we can go into next year all clear."

My, how very Californian! But it also sounded interesting. I thought it would be like a little game, something along the lines of making New Year's resolutions, but far deeper and more rewarding. During the ceremony he created, Robert helped me release something far more important than the desire to lose a few pounds, or go to the gym more often; he helped me to release all my limited thinking around whether I was worthy of being in a loving relationship, and whether I was allowed to have the dream life I wanted. It was beautiful.

Before returning to Los Angeles, Robert made a proposal—not a marriage proposal, but a relationship proposal. "What if we decide that we will be together for one year," he said, "That means we won't break up for a whole year, for any reason. And in that time we will give us our full attention. Even if we drive each other crazy, or whatever; even if something happens and we feel like we want to run away, we won't. We're going to stay together in the relationship for a year and see what happens."

"I do, I mean, I agree... We'll work it out," I said, "whatever comes our way." Robert liked that one.

And we did. We committed to our relationship for one year no matter what. We flew back and forth over the Atlantic and tried to visit each other as often as possible. Robert would come and stay with me for a week or so, I would go and stay with him for a week or so. We spoke on the phone each day, even if it was only five seconds to say, "I love you." The longest we were apart was five weeks in total.

I enjoyed going out to California, but suddenly I couldn't imagine myself living there, and Los Angeles often overwhelmed me. Mostly, I was concerned about Aspire and the practicality of moving the business across an ocean and to the other side of an entire continent.

One day, Robert and I were sitting in deck chairs on Will Rogers Beach in Santa Monica. It was a Wednesday afternoon, the wide-open white sand empty of people. Robert dozed off next to me as I gazed out at the ocean trying to figure out if, and how, I could live here. Suddenly in the waves directly in front of me, I saw a school of dolphins playing.

I nudged Robert, "Robert, look! Dolphins. It's marvelous!"

Robert didn't open his eyes, or miss a beat, "There are always dolphins here."

I wanted to live in California, the place where dolphins always play. A far cry from the council estate I grew up on.

Aspire would be fine.

Our long distance relationship wasn't always easy. There were times I thought Robert was so up there in the clouds it would drive me nuts, and he often thought I acted overly practical and too down to earth. In reality, though, we are the other's perfect complement. It was positive and rewarding to learn to understand each other and appreciate each other's differences, rather than seeing them as irritating, limiting, or not as good as our own qualities. Together, we were starting to define what a 'perfect' relationship looked like to us, and I started to learn how to let go of being Ms. Independent and Ms. Controlling in order to be in a quality relationship.

Making dreams a reality takes work. We must commit to our visions and follow them through. Many of us give up at the first hurdle, when what we thought was perfect seems flawed; or when we realize we have to make changes and it could be more difficult than we first thought. That's the time to look inside and ask yourself, "What is it I need to change or do differently to achieve my dreams?" It's the perfect time to adapt, think differently, and stay the course.

When we do that, dreams really do come true.

CHAPTER 14

The Queen & I

"I think the Queen invited me to lunch."

Robert sat in stunned silence on the other end of the line. It was 5 a.m. for him, in bed at home in California. I was in Brighton on the South English coast, meeting with my U.K. team, all part-time subcontractors. We were at the home of one of my coaches, Soraya.

"Well, not only me," I said, "me and 199 other women. It seems I've won an award. I'm one of the Top 200 Women to Impact Business and Industry."

"That's incredible, when is it?" He said, sleepily.

"February 14th. Valentine's Day."

He was quiet for a moment. It was going to be our first Valentine's Day and I hadn't seen him since he had gone home in early January. We planned to meet in Las Vegas where he was speaking at a conference.

"Well," he said, "sounds like I've been trumped by the Queen. Wow! Congratulations!"

Robert was supportive and wonderful. We talked over the invitation, supposedly hand carried by a courier from Buckingham Palace, and how exciting it would be to meet the royal family—that is, if it wasn't a joke being played on me. I couldn't seem to stop myself from thinking the Queen had it all wrong.

Aspire was going well enough for us to consider expanding our marketing and public relations. A big financial step, but we had prepared for the next level and we were ready. The purpose of meeting my U.K. team in Brighton that day was to discuss, among other initiatives, applying to be considered for an award or two so we could increase our profile and gain some recognition. The Queen beat us to the punch.

I partly thought my new assistant Gillian (the next Gillian in my life) orchestrated an elaborate practical joke, especially the bit about the invitation being hand-delivered to our City of London office from Buckingham Palace.

"It looks official enough," they told me from the office, "there's even a number to call to R.S.V.P."

What the hell. I dialed the number. This is it, I thought. If I hear one of my team members cackling on the other side of the line then I'll have a good laugh. Someone answered, something about Buckingham Palace, no cackling.

I blanched for a second, this was no practical joke. I really was to be honored by the Queen of England. I, the Sam Collins who grew up on a council estate with no money, was going to Buckingham Palace to stand eyeball-to-eyeball with the royal family. Still, at any point during this call, the Queen's staff member might say, "Oops!" they made a mistake, had the wrong Sam Collins, thanks, but no thanks!

But it didn't happen. The staff member gave me details on how to dress, how not to dress, when to arrive, where to go, and security protocols. My hands shook even as I hung up the phone. The event was still a few weeks away. There was one problem though, I didn't have a thing to wear.

And right up to the day before the luncheon, I still didn't have a proper formal dress. Aspire was at full-speed and I hadn't had a minute to myself in weeks and dress shopping, it must be said, even to meet the Queen, is never at the top of my priority list on any day of the week. Checking my 'to do' list for the day, I figured I still had plenty of time as the luncheon didn't start until 1:00 p.m. and I had more than 24-hours. I made my plan.

Plan A: Go for a run in morning. Catch the train to London, twenty minutes. Head to the shops on Oxford Street (off-the-rack is not a problem). Get ready at Julia's house (she lives near the Oxford Street shops). Cab to Buckingham Palace. Meet Queen.

"Piece of cake," I said, and started out my busy day.

The next morning I took my morning run and came home for a quick bite. After that, I shoved my makeup and everything I thought I'd need for the luncheon into my backpack and headed for the train wearing my running outfit; why shower twice?

The train from my house in Rickmansworth to Baker Street in London normally takes about twenty minutes. Except, at about five minutes into the trip, on the most important day of my life, the train stopped moving— the expression dead in its tracks taking on a whole new meaning for me.

One annoying bit of English railway trivia is when a train stops running, nobody seems to know when it will start again and there is no information available. Not only that, they don't let you off so you can walk someplace to catch a cab because, more often than not, you're out in the middle of nowhere, like on this particular day.

Fifteen minutes lugged by and the train sat silently on the tracks, and my Plan A started crumbling around me. You know the sinking feeling you get when you have an important appointment and you're stuck on a train? I sighed a lot; I shifted around impatiently, looking out the window at the green fields outside Rickmansworth; I checked my watch repeatedly, my mind racing to come up with a new strategy. Then I came up with Plan B.

Plan B: Directly to Oxford Street. Skip Julia's house. Short cab ride to Buckingham Palace. Meet Queen.

Yet another annoying bit of English railway trivia is the trains usually start up again without any announcement, you just start moving. This time, however, there was an announcement. The train was delayed. Really? They were working on it. They were sorry.

"Oh God!" I said, a little too loud. It wasn't looking good.

Plan C: If this bloody train ever starts up again, skip Oxford Street. Off at the next stop to find a dress shop. Longer cab ride to Buckingham Palace. Meet Queen.

Finally, after about fifteen long minutes the train started to move. Now feeling heavier than before, and so much slower. I did the thing you do when you're inside something that's not going fast enough—rocking back-and-forth in my seat, trying to make the train scoot faster down the track.

At last we arrived at the next station, Harrow-on-the-Hill, where the train driver announced it would be delayed again. I practically leapt from the train and ran straight up the steps to the shopping center and into the first dress shop I could find. It took roughly a minute to locate a dress, without any analysis of what would best express me—or time enough to try it on. Brown and gold stripes? Not my favorite colors but nice enough and it looked like it would fit.

"I'll take it!" I said, frantically shoving the dress over to the saleswoman. She stepped back, a little unsure of what I might do next.

When I walked back out to the street and back towards the station to get a taxi, I realized I had failed to include a critical piece of data in my last plan recalculation. Before me on the street was a sea of people, fellow passengers from the train I had exited, with the same idea as me, all trying to catch the same trickle of taxis running past this station.

Shit.

Plan D: Back on another train. Do make-up and hair on train. Tube to Victoria Station and short cab ride to Buckingham Palace. Meet Queen.

If you've ever tried applying liquid eyeliner on a bouncing train, it is not easy, but I'm here to say it can be done. As the train pulled into Baker Street, I was dripping a brand new layer of sweat over the top of the sweat from my earlier run. I was in London, but with one last connection still ahead of me, Victoria Station by way of the underground, and I still wasn't changed into my dress.

Plan E: Change in the public bathroom at Victoria Station. Short cab ride to Buckingham Palace. Meet Queen.

A bit of luck this time! There were no delays on the tube and I arrived at Victoria Station quickly. The station bathrooms looked as you might imagine—cracked, hazy mirrors, graffiti, various sundry smells, better than some, worse than most. I needed somewhere to change and slather make-up over my sweaty face. "Well, you do what needs to be done, Sam," I said to myself. "She's not going to know, it'll be okay." The more I thought about it, the funnier it was.

At last I made my way up to the street again, crowded with people, again after the same cabs. I checked my watch—twelve minutes. Shit, again.

Plan F: Run.

Victoria Station is a ten-minute walk from Buckingham Palace. I ran as fast as possible—legging it as we say in England; not a normal activity in formal dress wear and carrying a backpack. But six minutes later, I arrived at Buckingham Palace.

The palace buzzed with activity. Other honorees were arriving in beautiful cars and limousines, walking calmly into the ornate building. I made a quick primp of my hair and make-up, which surprisingly stayed put. I took a deep breath and skipped up to the palace gate, breathless and in the swoon of adrenaline.

"I'm one of the top 200 business women!" I said to the policemen at the gate. They looked me up and down, seeming more interested in the backpack slung over my shoulder than my crazy declaration.

One said, "Where's your invitation?"

You know the feeling you get when you want to produce something from a bag without looking inside? My first attempt produced a pair of tangled Marks and Spencer tights. The policeman did not seem amused.

"I know it's in here somewhere," I said, groping around as if the lights were out, and feeling a little panic it could be lost. I'm sure it was a matter of seconds, but it felt like ages. "Ta-da!" I said, the crumpled invitation in hand. The policeman was in no mood for amusements. In fact, I'm sure he inspected my invitation much more carefully than the others, even handing it over to his partner to inspect—it was obviously counterfeit. Finally, as if going against their better judgment, they let me in.

I wasn't even late!

I dropped off my backpack in the security area, straightened my dress, and took a look at myself up and down. Oh my God, I'd forgotten to change my shoes and I was still wearing my dirty, smelly trainers. I rushed back to the security and tore into my bag to find them. But in my rush, I had forgotten to bring, or buy, appropriate dress shoes.

My heart beat out of my chest, when the announcement rang out in the hall, and we were being called in. Fighting back the desire to leave and never come back, I took a deep breath. Okay, Sam, put on your I'm-meant-to-be-here-just-like-you face and all will be well. I deserved to be standing there with the other honorees, especially after that harrowing journey and, yes, even with incorrect footwear.

We were instructed by palace staff to walk single-file to meet Princess Anne, then Queen Elizabeth, then Sophie, Countess of Wessex, and a few other important dignitaries. As we lined up, someone else walked past giving all of us a crash-course in Queen Meeting: no bowing, don't nod, don't curtsy, definitely no touching, don't speak, wait until spoken to.

We shuffled toward our moment.

Inside the palace was beautiful, of course. I was as honored to meet the Queen as I was to be in the same room with these other women, the elite women of British business. I recognized a few in the line, women I had admired for years: Linda Bennett of L.K. Bennett, Jacqueline Gold of Ann Summers, Nicky Kinnaird of SpaceNK, and even Sharon Osbourne.

As I stood in the line, I daydreamed of when I was The Queen at school. I was 6 and it was The Queen's Silver Jubilee. It was marked with celebrations at every level throughout the country and Commonwealth. I never thought I would meet the actual Queen.

Suddenly, someone announced: "Samantha Collins from Aspire." And there I was looking at Princess Anne.

"I really love what you're doing with Aspire," she said with a great smile. Princess Anne is famous for doing her homework and remembering people. Still, I nearly fell over she knew anything about me.

"Thank you," I said.

I was shaking inside as I stepped once more and stood face to face with Her Majesty.

"Congratulations," said Queen Elizabeth, "well done." Her approving gaze then drifted from my eyes, to my dress, downward. When her eyes arrived at my feet, the Queen of England frowned.

Oh, God, I thought, she's going to tell me off about my shoes!

But the Queen didn't say a word, she retained her regal demeanor and looked toward the next honoree. My moment was over.

As soon as I was through the line of dignitaries, I sat at the first table I could find to try to hide my feet. Whew! It was all so topsy-turvy. I felt so honored to meet Queen Elizabeth and Princess Anne, it was one of the greatest accomplishments any Brit could hope for. To top it off, I spent the afternoon with some of the most powerful and successful women in the U.K., and was recognized along with them as being a positive force in my country.

Once it occurred to me that I was, in some way, on an equal par with all these wonderful women and nobody came to escort me out, I started to enjoy myself. In hindsight, I should have bought a dress much sooner. I had, quite literally, run to meet the Queen. No, I didn't drive up in a limo, and I didn't have on proper shoes, let alone a dress I would even have wanted to wear, but I was here and I was one of them, right where I ought to be.

After the luncheon I'd arranged to celebrate with some friends and clients who had stood by me since launching Aspire some six years earlier—my sister Emma, my friend Julia, Jeremy, the senior partner of the accounting firm BDO Stoy Hayward and my first corporate client, as well as a few of my own important dignitaries. I asked them to meet me back in The Albert Pub where I waitressed in 1996.

If someone from the future came to me one night in the pub, working in complete misery, and said, "Don't despair, Sam. In a few years you'll be honored by the Queen—in your running shoes, no less—and you'll have a successful business, an incredible man, and rather than come to work here for £3 an hour, you'll be celebrating on the other side of the bar," I would have had a good laugh in their face then probably told them to leave me alone. I couldn't have imagined any of it happening, not in a million years, and definitely not to me.

But eleven years later, I was a different woman. I had learned and mastered lessons about resilience in the face of setbacks, about confidence in myself, about having faith in what I was meant to do, about being proactive, and about creating my own destiny.

I couldn't have designed what had happened to me if I had wanted to. I certainly didn't make any proactive moves to get an award from the Queen, although I was conscious of telling everyone I met about what we were doing, because working hard was not enough and self-promotion, as unnatural as it felt, was also important. Yet, in any promotional activity, the only principle I have ever tried to follow is my simple business philosophy, which I try to maintain each and every day: Be a good person, work hard, and make a difference in the world.

The real reason it happened to me was because I was the right person to make it happen; I wasn't born the right person, I became her.

Receiving the award from the Queen was like the universe saying: If you have this award and this success you will be more visible to more women—it will help you make even more of a difference.

Always, Radio Heaven.

I realize the more credibility I receive, through awards and honors and success, the more likely people will be to work with Aspire, and the more women I can help to make a difference in the world.

As women, we often don't seek the spotlight; instead, we quietly get on with the hard work of getting the work done. It's our nature. Still, both the recognition and the leadership positions get starved away from us, while our male counterparts, who may be equally or less qualified, become the stars.

It is a myth that working hard is enough to be successful (according to research from gender think-tank Catalyst). Women, especially because it comes less naturally to us, must learn to advocate for ourselves, get good at doing our own P.R. work, and make sure we are known, too. Women who choose to step up and take the star role—not for the spotlight, but to satisfy their greater purpose—and women who dare embark on the journey of becoming themselves, rather than trying to act like someone else, or pretending they are a different gender, can achieve not only career success, but realize their potential to be a tremendous influence on the world.

Follow this philosophy: Be a good person, work hard, and make the biggest difference to others as you can and you will be recognized for it. Simple as it may sound, this is about developing a reputation for integrity, focusing on fundamentals, and having the bigger picture focus on more than yourself. It's not about a self-promoting P.R. campaign, it's realizing the more people know you, the bigger difference you can make.

What do you want to be known and recognized for in your life and work? Get clear on why is it important to you to develop this reputation—be specific. Then identify who you need to get out there and tell about your efforts. When you shine with both self-humility, confidence, and the knowledge that what you do is bigger than yourself, others will recognize you accordingly.

CHAPTER 15

One O'clock Deadline

One September day in 2007 during one of Robert's visits to me, we were lying in bed on the top floor of the Rickmansworth house doing nothing special. It was an ordinary day. Comfortable. Peaceful. Happy.

"Will you marry me?" he asked, just like that.

"But it's not even been a year into our experiment," I said, thrown for a pleasant loop.

He laughed, saying, "You didn't answer the question."

"Of course I will," I said, unable to stop smiling. Sam Collins, who nine months before had run away from love, had finally found her home.

Then he said, "So, do you think we might get on with that 'Desperately!' thing, then?"

I was surprised. Robert never had his own family and he was about to be 55-years-old. I guessed time was of the essence then and we had better get started! Later that day, ever practical me made an appointment with my doctor in Rickmansworth. I wanted to get a check up and get his okay for pregnancy.

"You're thirty five, Sam," the doctor said. "You'll have to give it a try. If you don't get pregnant in six months, come back."

We didn't have a long engagement, since we also wanted to get pregnant as soon as possible. In early November 2007, and exactly one year after we'd met in St. Louis, I flew out to California with the intention of living there and taking the next step in my life. I arrived on a Monday morning, and we drove straight to Beverly Hills to get our marriage license. I loved Robert taking me to Beverly Hills, having fun with it, and not settling for a procedure in some random city. It added a touch of glamour even though we didn't plan to have a glamorous wedding. We wanted it to be only us. We had both been married before, and the logistics and expense of flying everyone over for a fancy affair was out of the question, so we asked the clerk for the next available date for the ceremony, which was Friday. I already knew, even in my gut, that this was right for us.

Straight after getting our license, we talked rings. Robert wanted us to have beautiful rings to forever symbolize our love. He took me to a diamond jeweler in Downtown Los Angeles where we chose our matching designs together, to be specially made and ready by Thursday. I made sure mine also complimented my mum's antique diamond ring, which I still wore everywhere.

With our wedding date set and rings on order, Robert and I ate a celebration lunch at our favorite restaurant Back on the Beach in Santa Monica, a lovely little café where tables sit outside in the sand and you can look at the wide stretch of shore and sea and wiggle sand between your toes while you eat.

We were eating salads and playing with the sand between each other's toes when Robert suddenly exclaimed, "Ouch!"

I looked at him. "What happened? What's the matter?"

"I'm not thure," he said... or, sort of said.

"You're not thure?" I laughed aloud. Then he smiled and I saw the gap in his mouth where a tooth was only moments before. "Oh gosh, Robert! Are you okay?"

Robert has caps on some of his front teeth and one had popped off as he chewed, leaving a gaping hole in the middle of his mouth. He looked so funny, and I have to say it, not too attractive for once.

"I think you should get that sorted out immediately," I said, as a giggle escaped. "We're getting married on Friday!"

"I'm also speaking to the French Trade Commission this evening."

"Oh, my goodness. We need to find a dentist—like now!"

We called Robert's dentist from the table. He couldn't do anything about it until the next morning.

"Are you seriously going to speak to the French Trade Commission with that smile? It's horrendous!"

"Well" he said. "I don't want to let them down. Maybe I can make a joke of it."

That evening he left for his talk and actually did try to make a joke of it, but apparently this group did not find it even mildly amusing. They never asked him back. C'est la vie!

Thankfully, Robert managed to get a replacement tooth the next morning and go back to his old handsome self.

Wednesday morning, I woke up at about 5 a.m., a little tingly and queasy in my tummy. I'd known for a few weeks that I might be pregnant, since my period hadn't come and I was always as regular as a clock. I sneaked into the bathroom so I didn't wake Robert. I was nervous and I wanted to do it on my own, in case it was a false alarm. I opened the home pregnancy test kit, followed the instructions, and then spent an agonizing three minutes waiting.

"It's positive. I'm pregnant!" I yelled, running back to our bed and waking Robert.

"Fantastic!" Robert said, now fully awake. We lay in bed together for a while, extremely happy, cuddling and talking baby names. I phoned Emma since it was 1 p.m. in the U.K. She started screaming in the middle of the food aisle of Marks & Spencer in Rickmansworth.

On Friday, Robert and I drove down to the Los Angeles courthouse. After going through security at the entrance, we walked the several floors up and sat in the waiting area. Being pregnant made for frequent bathroom visits while we waited. While I was in the bathroom the clerk came out and announced: "Silverstone."

"Here," Robert said.

"And where is your wife-to-be?" he asked.

"She's in the bathroom."

He smiled and said, "Are you sure?" (Guess it's not uncommon for people to do a runner at the L.A. courthouse!)

Our wedding was only the two of us, without any witnesses. I was bloated and uncomfortable, already putting on pregnancy weight. As we trundled in, the judge asked if I would like flowers. Sure! Who wouldn't? He handed me a dusty bouquet made of purple plastic flowers. Robert and I both tried not to crack up laughing, as we had already been giddy for an entire day knowing we were pregnant too.

The ceremony lasted all of 30-seconds. Do you take this man? Yes. Do you take this woman? Yes. You're married... Next! We came out, really cracking up, laughing all the way to the car. We took a bunch of photographs making silly faces as we drove around the city, ending up in Long Beach at the R.M.S. Queen Mary, walking up and down the decks of the ship, carrying on and having fun. Rebecca, our Aspire Director of Programs, rang me on my cell to report in on one of the Aspire workshops she had delivered that day. I let her rave about how well it had gone before I surprised her with, "Well, I have more good news. I married Robert today!"

"What!" she said stunned, "Oh, Sam! Congratulations to you both! That's wonderful!"

We drove to Laguna Beach and spent the night in a lovely beachside hotel with the sound of the ocean waves crashing on the shore outside our window.

Marrying Robert truly was the best day of my life, and he filled my wedding day with everything I could ever want. I didn't need to have the dress, or the flowers, or the cake, or the big occasion. While I'm sure all of that is wonderful, I have never experienced it and I didn't need the promise of it; the only important thing was Robert and I were together, laughing and having the best time enjoying our day. That is what's fundamentally brilliant about our relationship, all that matters is being together, enjoying each other, and experiencing life with someone who loves you deeply and wants the best for you. It's a cliché that the most important things in life are free, but it's true. When you have a solid foundation of real love, accompanied by attraction, then you don't need any fluff.

As much as we can fear failure, we can also fear success. Dreams do come true, and we need to be ready to accept them, believe we deserve them, and be free to live them.

After we were married, Robert and I settled into life in California. It was a longtime dream of mine to work part-time, but I was a self-confessed workaholic with an ever growing to do list. For me, the concept of part-time was a pipe dream. I now lived 5,000 miles away from my business and my team: Rebecca, Carolyn, Yas, Anna and Janet—all living in the U.K. My worries about how I could make it thrive while growing a family and my marriage weighed heavily on my mind.

Robert had no changes to make. He had already spent twenty years as an executive and entrepreneur, and now happily worked from home, coaching businesses over the phone. He started work at 8 a.m. and finished by 1 p.m.

Every. Single. Day.

In fact, Robert would often finish work before noon, have lunch, and use the rest of the afternoon for reading, hiking, errands, enjoying the beach, fun—or whatever.

Whatever.

So when one day Robert really sprung it on me and said, "Can't you finish work at one o'clock, too?" I thought he had completely lost it.

It was a tall order. I was the poster girl for a twelve-hour workday, and happily so. I truly believed a prerequisite for building a successful business was a minimum twelve-hour day. I not only worked twelve hours a day, I worked six days a week, taking only Saturday off to relax with friends and family, and on Sunday it was right back to work. It was my schedule for years, and frankly, I was so passionate about what I do that those twelve hours flew by pretty quickly, and I always accomplished an enormous amount of work.

"That is not going to be possible," I said, "I have way too much to do..." and I proceeded to give him the laundry list of reasons why it was impossible for me: The volume of work I had took me past one o'clock. I had a different type of client. My clients were in Europe. Our businesses weren't the same. The other projects I had would take me way past one o'clock. In fact, it would be more stressful for me to try to finish by then, not less. "Thank you for offering, though."

Robert is nothing if not resilient, and over the next few weeks he kept asking me gently if I was ready. There was something truly insidiously attractive about his schedule, but I was the queen of justifying why it was a ridiculous idea—annoying even.

"When the time is right for you," he would say, "when you're ready, let me know."

Secretly, I wanted to finish working at one o'clock, who wouldn't? I was jealous, and a little resentful, when he would be done and go off to have fun without me, and I sat planted in front of my laptop. Of course I wanted to spend our afternoons together, but it seemed so impossible. There are many, many books written about time management, and I have read a lot of them, even taken classes from the authors, and still was unable to fathom how this could possibly work for me. One day, irritated that Robert was going to the beach without me yet again, I couldn't take it any longer. We sat down and discussed it.

"What's the worst that would happen if you stopped at one o'clock?" Robert said.

"My work wouldn't get done. I wouldn't make any money. I would be stressed. Eventually, Aspire would fail and I'd lose my clients. So, yeah, it would be terrible!"

Robert is a mentor and coach, too, so I braced myself for a session with his plethora of annoying time-management techniques, ways I could delegate my work, with a dash of "let go" mumbo jumbo for good measure. I had moved to a new country, I was already in panic about how to run a U.K. business from California, and I was not in the mood for training.

"Shall we try it?" Was all he said.

And all I could reply was, "I don't know."

"Well, do you want to try? Is this something that you would like to happen?"

"Yes," I said, "if we could find a way to make this work, of course I would love it."

"Well, let's try," he said. "Let's give it a trial period of two weeks, finishing at one o'clock California time." Which, he reminded me, was still 9 p.m. in England, long after normal people have finished work.

We proceeded with the plan. At five minutes to one, Robert poked his head around the door to tell me it was time. The first few times it looked like this:

"Five to one, time to finish, Sam."

"Go away!"

Then he changed strategy on me. "Get your beach clothes on, we're leaving in five!" Eventually, I complied and we ended up at the beach. He took me to our café in Santa Monica, and we sat enjoying coffee with our toes in the sand.

"How does it feel to be having lunch on the beach right now compared to working back at your desk?" Robert asked.

"Well, I'm really enjoying being here back on the beach," I said, suppressing my guilt.

"Are you stressed?"

"No. Not really," I realized with a bit of surprise.

"Is everything falling apart on you?"

"No."

And then I understood the only thing holding me back from implementing the One O'clock Deadline was me. I was the one setting all the limits around what I could and could not do, and I was the only person who could make it succeed or fail. We originally set our One O'clock Deadline test for two weeks, but soon it was two months, then four months, then six—and then it became how I worked every day.

I could never imagine going back.

My new schedule was 6 a.m. to 1 p.m., and, skipping lunch, it's pretty much a normal workday. I found everything I needed to do could be fit into seven hours.

My assistant, and right hand woman, Janet, and I work together over email every day. Janet is an extremely smart former-medical examiner who wanted to spend more time with her kids. When she was searching for a part time job and even considering working on the check out in Marks & Spencer in Rickmansworth, she had seen my little notice in the newsagent window. It was, and continues to be, a match made in heaven. Janet is the cornerstone that keeps everything running smoothly, and her own strong commitment to finishing on time helps me to do the same.

I started working with my clients over the phone, and empowering my team to deliver the workshops themselves in the UK. If work was left undone at the end of seven hours—always the case since there's no shortage of exciting projects—well then, it could wait.

Learning the power of not spreading myself too thin was a big deal. I'm passionate about my work and I'm the person who can do multiple projects at the same time, believing I can balance them all. I soon realized saying "Yes" to a lot of projects because they seemed interesting, or paid well, or I felt like I should because someone asked me to had never helped me be more successful. Soon I was only saying "Yes" to what I wanted to do. I could do a check-in with myself, take my "temperature" as I learned to put life first, then build work around life, rather than the other way around.

Many of us make the mistake of putting work first, including me, and then try to fit life into what's left. This has disastrous implications for our quality of life. What's more, no matter who you think you are, it could mean doing only B or C-grade work on ten moderately successful projects that keep you afloat, instead of doing an A-grade job on three or four projects that get you noticed and advance your goals.

When I started to take the opposite approach, I learned I could create a firm boundary around work: Monday through Friday only, weekends strictly for enjoying my husband and, soon enough, my kids. It was going well and I was grateful to rest, as I was now getting bigger with my pregnancy.

I should have suspected it wasn't going to be enough for Robert.

"Wouldn't it be nice," he said, one day when I was about six months pregnant, "if we could take Fridays off? I mean, you know, not work at all on Friday."

I mean, you know, no!

This suggestion actually made me angry, and I responded exactly the same way as I did when he introduced the One O'clock Deadline, with something like, "You have to be joking! You asked me to stop work at one o'clock, I did it. I stopped working Sundays, of my own accord. Now you want me to give up Fridays? No."

Today, I understand that my anger was driven by fear. If I took Fridays off, too, clearly everything would fall apart. Back then, I thought I was right, and he was nuts.

"We can try it. Let's try Fridays together and see what happens," he said, calmly.

Same journey, different day.

Robert said vacations didn't need to be for weeks and we should treat the day like we were on holiday. A holiday every week? Who could resist? We renamed Friday our Daycation, and spent the entire day together; a walk in the Santa Monica mountains, breakfast at the beach, an early movie, a late lunch, anything to spend the whole day together as a couple, getting to know each other more deeply, laughing, and talking.

After a couple of those, of course, I never wanted to work another Friday again. It gave me something to look forward to all week and still does.

I speak from experience, we can get so caught up in our schedules, especially when we're passionate about the work we do, but it is driven by fear and nothing else. I have to work. I have to earn money. The whole world's going to blow up. I'll starve my family. I won't be able to pay my mortgage. When we're in the thrall of those kinds of fears, and you know what those fears feel like, we so easily forget how remarkable life can be. We forget how wonderful it is to go for a walk with someone, talking, and spending time together.

There is so much more to life than working it away.

One way to handle work is to put inviolable lines in the sand around our time, refusing to listen to our own self-defeating crap. Also, stop reading time management books or thinking it's all too hard and doesn't apply to your situation. It's all in your mind. Once we realize that we are responsible for how we live our lives, the shift happens all on its own. Like Robert says, all you really have to do is try it.

For me, the proof came within a single year of starting the One O'clock Deadline and taking Fridays off, during which Aspire's revenue increased by twenty percent. But the real benefit of making this shift was that I stopped being a control freak. My stress level dropped and my happiness level climbed, and much more than twenty percent! I had micro-managed my team in England for years, but soon realized it took up way too much time, both for me and for them. When I learned to pull back, I told them: "Look, you are all good, and you know what you are doing. You do the workshops the way you want and if you ever need my input, ask."

Everybody involved was empowered by the decision, and my team felt freer to take on their own initiatives. A happy team is a more productive team, and productivity resulted in higher performance, and my revenue proved it. By gaining more free time, I ended up making more money.

Funny how that works.

Of course, some people say the only reason I achieved this freedom, is because I have the flexibility of running my own business. This is true, and at the same time, not. Running your own business often requires working far more hours than I ever did as an employee, and I maintained a six-day, twelve-hour plus per day schedule for a solid six years. It was only when I realized my choices were entirely in my mind that I was able to significantly reduce my working hours and remain successful.

Within the business world, women are increasingly making the decisions and there are growing options for working part-time or flexi-time. Unfortunately, the option often comes along with a reduction in pay, relegation to less exciting work, and the perception you are somehow less committed. To top it off, women are still paid less than men for doing the same job. This must change for women to be encouraged to try for the most senior positions, where the business world desperately needs them. Younger women in particular need role models, senior women who openly work flexibly and part-time and are still well paid. My advice is to lobby for highly paid, challenging, part-time positions within your organization, and if it's not happening, find or start a company where it is.

I have 28 hours of time allotted over four days to dedicate to business. (I don't call business "work" because having kids is also a lot of work!) From there I ask myself: "What will be the best use of my time this week?" As opposed to my old question: "What do I need to do next?" These are two radically different questions; the first one led me to big-picture, strategic use of time, while the second one kept me down in the weeds doing everything.

Create strong boundaries and protect your family time at all costs. It takes practice and discipline and dealing with your fears. For me it was so worth it, and I strongly encourage you to imagine the possibility for yourself.

What does your ideal work week look like? When are you working? When are you playing? What are the limiting beliefs holding you back from achieving it? Don't take a time-management approach but a time-leadership approach: design your life first, and then allocate your work time around it. What decisions or actions do you need to make to achieve your ideal time/life balance?

Overcome your fears and develop a positive mental attitude towards time. Don't you think it's about time?

CHAPTER 16
Earthquake Jake & Halloween Charlie

According to Aspire research, over 50% of working women have children. For these women 'sheer workload' and 'balancing work and home' are their top challenges. Before I had children I already faced major challenges with time. When I gave birth to my boys, all hell broke loose. I realized quickly why the word is boisterous, not girl-sterous!

On July 29th, 2008, I was a substantial eight and a half months pregnant. I wish I could say I'm one of those women who enjoy being pregnant. I do not. I was mostly miserable and overate as compensation for my misery, blooming to a robust 200 pounds and then some. It was a beautiful sunny morning and I sat on the sofa at home in our living room to do some work. I balanced my laptop on my tummy and typed away, when suddenly I felt the sofa move. Then, a moment later, the rest of the room followed. It was as if the entire house rose and crested over an enormous wave at the beach. What on earth is that? I thought.

Robert bounded out of his office at the front of the house, shouting, "Welcome to your first California earthquake!"

"I don't feel so good," I told him.

"Oh, it's no big deal," he said, looking around at the ceilings and running his fingers over the wall. "See? No damage. These tremors can be jarring, but that one was pretty mild. Fun, eh? You don't get that kind of a ride in England!"

"That's not what I mean," I said, giving him The Look. He immediately took the hint, gathered me up, and sped us to the hospital.

"This is your first child?" said the delightfully Scottish nurse checking us in.

"Yes," I said, adding, "and we're going drug-free."

"Give it an hour or two, love," said the Scottish nurse. Love—funny how hearing a little English term comforted me, and how quickly it could evaporate as she smiled and said, "Let's see how you feel in an hour or two."

I had already done deep research, of course, and knew it wasn't good for the baby or me to be loaded up with drugs during birth. The hypno-birthing weekend course Robert and I attended opened our eyes to new and less traditional ways of giving birth. Caitlin, who we asked to be our birth doula (meaning "mothers help") for my labor, ran the class. I also discovered who was to blame for the way most Western women give birth today. Good old King Henry VIII one day decided women shouldn't give birth standing, as they had done for as long as women gave birth, because he imagined it should be much more dignified to lie down on a bed.

Typical.

For me, lying on my back was far more uncomfortable than walking off the contractions. So I walked. And walked. And walked. Around and around the halls of the Kaiser Permanente, Woodland Hills hospital. Robert was the perfect partner for this new journey: he walked with me, comforted me, talked me through contractions and wrote down the times in a little note pad. After twelve hours of walking, resting, and walking, I gave birth standing, like many African women do, and like women through all history have done.

Robert stood directly in front of me, looking into my eyes, his hands gently on my shoulders the entire time as I held on to him. As each contraction came, he would count me through it, and as he did, he would encourage me gently saying, "You're so powerful and calm," or "you're serene and strong." The only time I had pain was when the nurses took Robert away from me hourly to check my heartbeat—and it was agonizing pain for those brief minutes. But as soon as Robert came back and our eyes were locked together, the pain evaporated. What an incredible experience in connection, and in the power of the mind!

At 4:52 p.m. on July 30th, 2008 our first son Jake, named for my mum's maiden name, Jagar, was born completely drug-free. Little Jake stayed alert and awake right away and so were we. He was our Earthquake Jake.

"I want to shake your hand," my doctor said as he checked me out after the birth. "Nobody has drug-free births these days. Congratulations!"

That first night with Jake in the world was my introduction to the highs and lows of motherhood. Holding him in my arms and looking into his beautiful tiny eyes, filled with unconditional love, was a feeling I wish I could bottle and give to every single person on this planet. Such pure love is a precious gift, and Jake, Robert, and I would have this wonderful bond to last our whole lives. I gazed at my new baby dreamily.

And then he started to scream.

The nurses looked at me, winked, and wished me luck. Who knew such ear piercing wails could come from such a tiny mouth? I realized right away that I had a huge personality on my hands. I rocked him and sang him Que Sera Sera like my mum had done with me.

A few days after we had taken Jake home, our friend Diana, who studies Astrology, came over and did his chart for us. "Jake has strong leadership capability," she said.

"Hey, wonderful!" I said.

"But you'll have to direct him well and help him develop his values."

Okay...

"... because this leadership capability could either be, like, a strong ethical CEO, or possibly a gang leader."

Say what?

I'll always remember that moment because it helped me to understand what Jake needs from me. His presence in my life was to help me develop my love, patience, organization, and stress management skills to their fullest. When he was two-weeks old, I dreamed one night he graduated from university in the U.K. and he was receiving a prize for his contribution to racial equality. The dream was so completely vivid. I remember standing in the audience, madly clapping with pride for his achievement. "That's my boy!" I thought, beaming.

When I awoke the next morning, I single-mindedly determined to be the best possible role model I could be. My biggest challenge and most exciting project to date: being both a role model mum and successful businesswoman at once.

One concept that relieved me early on was asking for help—not always an easy concept for us women, and particularly difficult for high achievers. Getting help was something I rarely ever did. The One O'clock Deadline already taught me about that "default belief" I held, that I could do everything by myself, and the high price I had paid to hold on to it. I wasn't sure about hiring a nanny. My worries ranged from having a stranger in the house looking after my child on up to the expense of childcare, but I was sure Robert and I couldn't do it alone. I wanted to continue working and I wanted to raise Jake, and while Robert was determined to be as hands-on a dad as possible, his schedule still required a lot from him and frequently exhausted him—after Jake came Robert lost weight even faster than me.

After a few months, our nurturing and straightforward nanny Jay came into our lives. This larger-than-life Afro-Caribbean woman in her late-twenties arrived for the interview with purple streaks in her hair and tattoos everywhere, and a wealth of experience. I loved her right away, and she has taught us more about parenting than any book or course ever could, one of the unexpected bonuses of hiring an experienced nanny.

By degrees we settled into our routine: Robert and I working from home each morning (only to 1 p.m., of course!) and Jay looking after Jake. Thank goodness for mute-button technology on telephones! Earthquake Jake earned his nickname and we hardly slept for months. I learned how to operate on a couple hours of sleep and often power-napped in between client sessions on the phone.

We all travelled back to the U.K. together every 6 weeks, so I could deliver workshops and attend to my clients. During those trips we would leave Jay in L.A. and stay in the Rickmansworth house, where I worked during the day while Robert looked after Jake, and we would trade off in the evenings so Robert could do his Californian client sessions by phone, since they were eight hours behind us.

I had two jobs during the day—job one: portray a motivational speaker and facilitator who knew what she was doing, and job two: pump as much breast-milk as possible. Both jobs were a challenge. I remember being in the bathroom of one of my corporate clients in London sitting on the toilet with the lid down, the whirring of the pump reverberating off the tile floors and walls. I was always vaguely embarrassed, hoping no-one would hear, until one day a woman in the stall next to me asked, "Is that the Medela double pump? Tell me... how is it?" Pumping breast milk in the restroom: one more unique facet of being a woman in business. Let's accept it!

Our bi-continental work life may have sounded like fun and glamour, but travel with a baby while keeping two businesses going took its toll. I needed more support and I envied those friends with mothers and grandmothers to help them. One day when Jake was a few months old, Robert announced his sister Michele was coming to stay. I couldn't think of anything worse. Michele was ten years older than Robert and I didn't know much about her, at first, except she was happy Robert had finally married a nice Jewish girl. She'd left Manchester to settle in Toronto, and I half-assumed she was coming exclusively to check whether or not I was proper Jewish marriage material and how well I was handling it all.

She arrived immaculately dressed, armed with gifts for all, and straightaway set about to make my life a living heaven on earth! It was so unexpected and so wonderful. The best thing about Michele was she could always make me laugh until my belly hurt, the next best thing was she called me her new Sista. She reminded me of my mum so much I often had a mixture of heart-longing and astonishing comfort. Whenever she wasn't cooking up scrumptious meals or caring for my boys, Michele lay by the pool soaking up every possible moment of California sun, slathered in the same Ambre Solaire lotion my mum always used. I would get a whiff of the coconut fragrance and, if I squinted, I could imagine Mum. I would often fantasize about her coming over to California to help me with the kids, like mums do, and in so many ways, Michele became the mum I had missed for so long. I love her so much.

Six months and four transatlantic flights after Jake was born, we tried for a second baby. This sounds crazy after what I've written, but the "Big 4-0" was looming over me and since I was already sleep deprived, I figured it couldn't get any worse. Most of all, I wanted Jake to have the gift of a sibling as close in age as Emma and me.

We were extremely lucky, and I was pregnant again within two months. By this time I was seriously sleep deprived, and seriously grumpy, the sole reason being that Jake didn't like to sleep. Time flies and the One O'clock Deadline flew right out of the window. Everything in my life came down to feeding, getting sleep, and keeping Aspire afloat. Hormone and guilt levels were both running high; I finished every day in a heap of exhaustion, even with the help.

About five months into my second pregnancy, I said to Robert, "This baby's going to be different. This one will be more calm, I think."

"How do you know?" he said.

"I'm not sure how I know, somehow I just know. This baby is going to be different... and we need it to be different, too."

"What do you mean?" he said.

"I can't go on working this way. In fact, I can't face the prospect of traveling back and forth to England with two small children." Yet, I wondered, how would I keep Aspire going without travel? It's based in England, for heaven's sake.

"I have an idea," Robert said, in that certain way when he's about to challenge my thinking again. "Let's not travel for a whole year after the baby is born."

Say what? I couldn't imagine this even remotely working, but I was so deliriously sleep deprived at the moment that I was willing to ignore the possibility that our income could go away. I was willing to give it a go because, frankly, I needed more sleep! I missed our afternoons and Fridays together, not to mention that I was beginning to question my ability to both work and have children.

On Halloween 2009, I had just demolished four iced cinnamon buns and was sitting, ironically, in a parenting class with Jay on helping your child sleep better, a class I had missed with Jake and was determined to take before the new baby arrived. I announced to the group, "I'm so glad I made it to the class today, this time before I give birth!" No sooner did the words leave my mouth did my water break—three and a half weeks early. I stayed still, motioned to Jay, and remained seated until everyone had left the room. She then shuffled me out in wet pants, to the room next door, where Robert was attending a parenting class with Jake. I motioned to Robert from the window, but he didn't get it, gesturing five minutes with his hand. I waited, of course, no rush to get to the hospital this time around, after all, and it was a long drive back from Hollywood to Woodland Hills.

He came out with Jake, saw my wet clothes, and herded us all into the car. It's a myth that women need to rush off to a hospital because the whole process takes forever. So we drove home somewhat leisurely, made a sandwich, took showers, and left Jay at home with Jake as we drove to the hospital at 3 p.m.

The same Scottish nurse was there to admit us. "Second baby," she said, adding with a wink, "you sure took your time! No drugs again, right?"

"Right!"

This time around it was a bit more surreal. It was Halloween night and the place was decorated to the gills with ghosts, witches, and haunted houses, not to mention the nurses and doctors were dressed up in costumes—a sugar plum fairy and a witch helped us into our room.

Robert and I were geared up for the hours of long walks up and down hallways, all the reassuring, all the pain when the nurses came to check our heartbeats and, of course, counting through contractions. We were prepared for another marathon like Jake's birth. After a visit to the cafeteria for another iced doughnut, along with a quick oath that it would be my last one, we settled in and I fell asleep.

Slightly after midnight I awoke to my first big contraction. Robert jumped into action and I took a deep breath. He counted: "Ten, you are powerful… Eleven, you're serene… Twelve, doing so good, sweetheart…" He made it all the way to seventeen when I told him to shut up. I was in no mood for it. I made it through two more counts in my head, to nineteen, and nearly passed out from the intense and excruciating pain. Then there were three pushes and Charles, named after Robert's grandmother Charlotte, was born on November 1st, 2009—three years exactly after Robert and I met for the first time in St Louis. Quick, easy, and three and a half weeks early; we nicknamed him Halloween Charlie. The nurses gave him a different nickname—Buddha Baby. It's was apt. Charlie is still, to this day, like a calm sea washing over all of us during the day. His blue eyes and smile light up the room, and he is clearly the perfect complement to Jake's spirited tenacity.

Unlike his big brother, Charlie slept easily and hardly ever cried. He was so compliant, and I was so emotionally prepared for another Jake and his booming earthquake of a personality, that I asked the doctor to check him out again. The doctor handed Charlie back and said, "You have what we call..." I braced myself, "... a good baby."

Okay, new concept!

I am completely and utterly in love with my boys, and completely and utterly exhausted by them each and every day. It didn't escape me that I was doing all of this career work to advance women in the world, while being completely surrounded by men, and I was loving it!

We didn't go back to England for an entire year after Charlie was born. We recommitted to the One O'clock Deadline and Friday Daycations again. Many times, we would use our Fridays to sleep and get ready for a full weekend with the kids. None of it would have been possible without a strong mindset, and Jay.

My next big realization came in 2010, the year Aspire had its first million-dollar year, our highest revenue up to then. My belief was if I worked less, I would make less money, especially after having children, but nothing could truly "keep me" from having the life I wanted, except for me. What it came down to in the end was working smarter, not harder, and the biggest difference was putting life and family ahead of work.

Having children and the achievement of "Desperately!" have been the most wondrous gifts in my life so far. I love my relationship with my kids, and defend it fiercely. It is fundamentally important to me to be in their lives, and be a daily role model for them. I will not stand for a life where I don't watch them growing up because I'm doing business. Before Jake and Charlie were born I read an article in The Guardian newspaper which profiled a successful businesswoman proud of the fact she, "still put her kids to bed once a week." I swore this would never be me. I nearly always put my kids to bed myself. Yes, it is exhausting at the end of the day, and yes, I practically collapse into bed at night. But I plummet into my pillow with a giant smile on my face, knowing I've made a difference in my business, but more importantly to those two young souls to whom I have a responsibility to nurture into conscious men.

Having children is a significant life event, and the most challenging one. The biggest advice I can offer is to design your life around your family at its best. Get the most support possible, not abdicating responsibility to someone else, but having a team around you, both personally and professionally, helping you to stay sane, be a role model, and spend wonderful quality time with your kids.

It helps enormously that Robert and I have chosen to "co-parent" and support each other. I didn't see much of my dad growing up since he worked every day to support us. I'm glad to know this will not be our children's experience. Like me, Robert works from home and is as active in bringing up our boys as I am. He finds this to be just as rewarding and exhausting as I do, but neither of us would have it any other way.

The key is not to try to do it all. Stick to your boundaries, find the support, and create the balance that looks right for you and your family together.

CHAPTER 17

Getting M.A.D.

Making A Difference (M.A.D.) outside your regular work is a fundamental element of personal fulfillment for women, and is part of our responsibility for future generations and the planet as a whole. We can all make a difference. Women in business are highly philanthropic, with 86% giving to organizations they are passionate about, and their activity has increased to the tune of more than $15 billion annually since 1996 (Business and Professional Women's Foundation, 2007).

Each year at Aspire, we perform a survey with old clients and new, along with the women on our mailing list. One of the standard questions is: What motivates your work? Every year one of the top three answers is: Making a difference.

From the early days of Aspire I had a large group of women connected to us who were passionate about making a difference; and yet, we weren't doing anything with them when we could so easily be doing something. When this occurred to me in 2010, the world hung in a global recession and corporations were cutting back on spending. Was now the right time to think about giving back? Did I need to add something more to my plate? Wasn't there enough going on?

I looked at a few other foundations doing good work like Nike, The Body Shop, and Microsoft, but rationalized that they were different, special; and anyway, a lot bigger and better funded than Aspire. "Come on, Sam," said the little voice, "those are large companies that have been established for a long time. How can you possibly compare to them, or start a foundation?"

One afternoon Robert suggested I give myself an hour off to watch some television and put my feet up after I had complained all morning about how tired and achy I felt. I didn't put up a fight, shuffling into the family room and plopping down in front of the T.V.

I paused on a CNN special report about women in Afghanistan and was instantly captivated by the story of a poor woman making her way to a birthing center, through mountainous terrain and on the back of a donkey. The reporter said one in seven women in Afghanistan died in childbirth, which was both heartbreaking and mind boggling. This poor woman was trying to make her way over mountains to have her baby, and here I was sitting in a lovely house in sunny California, a wonderful family, a terrific husband by my side, and owner of a profitable business. Who was I to be complaining about my life?

Hang on.

I might have escaped reality and switched the channel over to the Unreal Housewives of Somewhere-or-Other, slipping further into a depressing torpor. While it's not unusual to watch discouraging stories on the news, what is unusual is when it actually hits home with you, and this report hit me particularly hard. This was a Radio Heaven moment coming over the television. I love those moments. They don't happen often, but when they do, I pay attention.

Something deep in my heart changed. I started to cry, realizing the woman's desperation. Imagine how any woman could be in such a despairing situation in today's world; how helpless must it feel. As sad and sorry as I was, I didn't have the first clue what to do about it, and I made about fourteen excuses why I shouldn't do anything about it at all.

I turned the T.V. off and Googled "women in Afghanistan" and up came a charity called Women for Women International. I clicked on the link and read all about this organization, which helps survivors of war in Afghanistan, Iraq, and Rwanda. They developed leadership programs to empower women in these countries to take leadership positions in their communities. I loved how they were working on the leadership aspect, because that's what we were doing at Aspire, only they were non-profits located in countries ravaged by war.

I emailed a quick note telling them what Aspire was all about, and asked if there was a way we might be able to help. Within a few minutes the president of the organization, Andree Simon, emailed back.

She wrote simply: "Let's talk."

The next day we did. It was a great phone call, and we formed a powerful connection. I asked her what the organization truly needed.

"We need more funding, of course," she said, "but our country directors and the staff in D.C. and London need mentoring, and coaching, and help with management skills."

"Really?" I said. "That's the same as in the business world."

"Yes, the same exact issues in a different environment."

"How many people are we talking about here?"

"Around 150, I guess."

I didn't have the capacity on my team to work with that many people, and I admitted as much.

"Well, what ideas do you have? What might you be able to do right now?" she said. And just like that we were in a brainstorming session.

"Well, I wonder about some of our clients, senior businesswomen who could be mentors for you. They're extremely smart, they're at the top of their organizations, and they deal with these issues all the time. They could mentor some of the younger women, your country directors, your managers, or even leaders in the organization. I'm wondering if we could set up a pro-bono mentoring between our clients who could become mentors and your female employees who could be mentees."

Bingo!

So in early 2010, when Charlie was three months old, we officially launched the Aspire Foundation, based on one idea: women supporting women, merging the corporate business world with the non-profit world, both learning from each other. To keep myself accountable and on track, I set a bold ambition to positively impact the lives of one million women and girls by 2015.

I set about the work of designing a free mentoring program where women applied to Aspire to become either a mentor or a mentee. It was a minimum commitment of six-months, one-hour per month by phone. Unexpectedly, many of the mentors spent even more time volunteering because they had formed strong bonds with their mentees.

The next step was promotion. It was easy for Women for Women International, because all they had to do was advertise it to their women, and before we knew it, they had brought us fifty mentees, ready to go. The next part was up to me. I sent an email to women in the Aspire community, explaining why and how to become a mentor.

Janet, my assistant in the U.K., sent our first mailing at 8 a.m. U.K. time. When I woke up in California the next morning and started my computer to check on responses, I was hoping for at least fifty mentors to meet the balance of mentees coming from Women for Women International. I held my breath and watched my inbox fill up with over one hundred mentor applications—and that was only the first day. What a thrill! It only affirmed we were doing exactly the right thing.

It has only grown since then. We now have Liesl, our virtual assistant, who manages the applications remotely from her home in Topanga, California. So far over 2,000 mentors and mentees from over 80 different countries have participated. Interestingly, we've always had roughly the same number of mentors as mentees, almost like someone is looking out for us somewhere. We have never experienced a big glut of mentors or of mentees, it's always balanced itself out in a matter of days.

In each six-month period, we ask our mentees to give us an estimate of the number of women they believe have been impacted through the mentoring. By February 2013 we estimated 541,000 women and girls, bringing us over halfway to our goal.

Wow!

I don't tell this story to say, "Look at me. I run a foundation now. Aren't I fantastic?" I tell it because I want you to be familiar with how a simple, low cost idea can become something grand, meaningful, and influential to the rest of the world. The simple and easy ideas—and the ones connected to our hearts—are the ones we often ignore because we think they're too simple or too easy. I believe, however, these kinds of ideas usually work the best and have the most impact.

There is one question on the mentoring application that I always read the response to: Why do you want to join the Aspire Foundation? More often than not, the answer is: I was always looking for a way I could give back without having to quit my corporate job or take too much time. In the Western world, even our simplest ideas can have a massive ripple effect of change, as long as we think bigger and join together with other like-minded people.

Making a difference has varying definitions for people, of course, but I wonder what it means to you. What benefit would making a difference have for you and others around you? What could you do to make more of a difference today in the causes you believe in?

It is our responsibility to do this. Yes, it gives us personal fulfillment, but more importantly, the world needs women like you and me to make a difference right now. We can do it easily, and giving true help has far more impact than simply giving money. If we can empower women to develop their leadership capabilities and make a bigger difference, the world will change for the better. The world is changing now because of our work and I'm so incredibly proud of that—what can ignite a fire in you?

CHAPTER 18

Baby Room to Board Room

I jumped right back into work the day after my boys were born. It may seem strange, but the truth was more ironic; working was a much-needed rest from the boys. I could escape to my desk off the kitchen while the kids were napping, and work on something I could control, something I was good at. I would work at odd times during the day and night and sleep was a rare commodity.

Work was far easier than looking after the boys, and still is, as stress in my business cannot compare to nursing every three hours, or trying to get Jake to sleep, or constantly keeping toddler Charlie from crawling into something he shouldn't—or worse, having them both screaming in unison. Going to the bathroom, having a shower, or eating a sandwich became enormous daily feats to accomplish.

Running Aspire was easy by comparison.

I had a great perspective shift. I used to think having kids couldn't be nearly as hard as running a business. After all, what's changing diapers, giving baths, and making sure they eat on time? What's so hard about that? But stress, sleep deprivation, and worrying over being out of control, or of being a failure, make mothering truly difficult. When you ask someone to do something at work, they usually do it. Not so in parenthood. Negotiation is a key element, along with juggling roles as a protector, teacher, psychologist, comforter, and loving presence in the face of defiance, or fear, or both at once. All of that is the hard part.

Mothering didn't come naturally and I found myself irritated, tired and deflated most of the time. I know I've said it already, but I was so tired that it made me lose my confidence. I doubted myself, my abilities, and I worried constantly, barely holding it together. Those first few months with Charlie in the world became a blur of nearly automated monotony. What I didn't realize all along was that I had been honing valuable leadership skills like patience, compassion, organization, and negotiation.

Robert said to me once, "if you can get broccoli into Jake's mouth, then you can convince a board of men to do anything."

He was right. Why didn't I think of that? In fact, being a parent should give you continuing education credit in business and leadership.

My journey being both a mother and a businesswoman began. I found myself using examples of my own children to help my female clients overcome their challenges and finding solace in other women with the same parenting challenges as me. It helped me understand and find practical strategies for my female clients at the most senior levels of their companies, who were also mothers.

I quickly realized the outdated attitudes many companies have in regards to working mothers. It's painfully irritating.

We've all heard of, or experienced, the P.M.S. (Pre-Menstrual Syndrome) symptoms women endure in the form of uncomfortable cramping and irritations before that time of the month. But there's another type of P.M.S. that is just as unpleasant—worse, in fact—affecting working men and women all over the world. I'm talking about the P.M.S. that stands for Pale, Male, and Stale, which describes the dinosaur generation of men, and even a few culpable women, running some of the biggest organizations, governments, and businesses around the world. Unfortunately, this crowd is responsible for the direction of the world in spite of a new generation who wants change. There are many difficulties for women in organizations where the senior level is P.M.S and there is an inherent bias against a certain way of being in business: a female way of being. There is a resistance to the more collaborative, democratic, and people-focused ways of doing business, particularly when it comes in the form of a woman.

When Jake and Charlie were four and three, I came across a panel discussion advertised online featuring senior CEO business leaders— men whom I admired. I noticed, however, that there were no women on the panel. So I emailed the man running the panel and asked where the gender balance was. I wasn't aggressive about it, I simply asked why there weren't any women on the panel.

"Would you be on the panel?" they responded.

"Sure!" It wasn't exactly my intention but, okay, why not? I wanted to see a woman on the panel and if it wasn't going to be someone else, it may as well be me. So I accepted the invitation.

On the night of the event, Jay came over to babysit. I dressed up and Robert came along for moral support. We arrived at the event as it was about to start and I was headed to the stage when a man in the audience came up and said, "I see they were looking for a pretty girl, so they put you on the panel."

Where's a banana when you really need one?

I experienced almost violent revulsion at this ridiculously unconscious and sexist remark. I smiled and said with more than a little bite, "Do you realize that's an inappropriate comment?"

"But," he said, oblivious and a bit flummoxed, "but I was giving you a compliment."

"Then first of all, thank you for the compliment," I said. "Thank you for saying I'm pretty. Now, are you saying the reason I'm on the panel is only because I'm pretty?"

"N-n-no."

"I should hope I'm on the panel because I have something more to say, than 'Hi, I'm pretty.' But maybe you'd rather say I'm pretty smart?"

"Yes. That's exactly what I'm saying," he said, now appropriately adjusted in his attitude.

This man was a nice man. I know he was a good person inside, and he probably didn't mean to be inappropriate. From his point of view, he was complimenting me. This is a perfect example of P.M.S. entrenched thinking. He didn't realize the demoralizing effect his unconscious comment could have had. What he said did throw me and make me a little angry, I trembled a little as I walked up to the stage. But it also encouraged me in a funny way—instead of trying to impress everyone by saying the "right" words, I said exactly what I thought. I gave my opinion. And you know something? It was received!

It was a terrific evening. I was particularly impressed by the CEO of Patagonia, Casey Sheahan, who was asked about the most important skills in business and declared love!

He proved to me that men can show their feminine side and be hugely successful too. The feedback on all of us in the panel was remarkable. A number of women came up to me at the end of the event and congratulated me for being brave and authentic. Another great advance!

The P.M.S. crowd reminds me of dinosaurs indeed. Dinosaurs once ruled the world and then one day they were killed off by a big climactic event, and now they're extinct. The P.M.S. crowd still rules the world, but their way of thinking is becoming extinct. The world is different now, and it's time to accept the change.

According to the Best Companies for Leadership survey, the top twenty organizations are almost twice as likely as the other 1,000 companies surveyed to have a high proportion of women in senior leadership positions. The Hay Group study of 45 outstanding women executives from large multinationals including IBM, Pepsi, and Unilever, when compared with a peer group of effective male executives and less effective women, found the 45 women knew when to be more nurturing, inclusive, and collaborative. The less effective women and men surveyed tended to rely primarily on the masculine styles of communication.

Feminine leadership recognizes the whole person and the existence of life outside of work. It is leadership founded on gut instinct and intuition and tuning in to what is needed holistically, instead of only in terms of profits and productivity. Being truly connected to our experience as wives, daughters, mothers, and friends allows us to understand leadership in a different way, a more conscious and evolved way.

What can you do to promote authentic leadership in your life and work? Be an authentic leader. Become aware of yourself as a whole woman, across all your contrasting roles; portray your own unique style and strengths, and how they benefit you, others, and your organization. Trust what you really think and never be afraid to say it.

CHAPTER 19

A Lesson in Resilience

"If you could live anywhere in the world, where would it be?" I said to Robert over dinner at Roy's Restaurant on Topanga Canyon Boulevard one evening.

He didn't skip a beat, "I would live and die in Topanga."

Topanga is more like a village than a city. Close to downtown Los Angeles but only a ten-minute drive from the ocean. It's a little enclave in the Santa Monica Mountains, eclectic and wonderfully politically incorrect. The word topanga when translated from its Chumash Indian roots means above the sky or heaven. When it comes to Topanga, the feelings get extreme. You either love it or hate it. Robert loved it. I hated it.

"I'd like to live in Topanga, too, if it wasn't so mountainous," I said for diplomacy's sake. "I can't see me living on a mountainside, and I really don't know how it would work with little kids. It's not practical to me."

"Fair point," he said, "but not every area of Topanga is on a mountain. There's a neighborhood called Old Canyon. It's flat, has a nice green park area that's great for kids. There's even a cool little community there, too. I think you'd probably love it."

"A flat lot in a community that's great for kids... in Topanga?" I said, thinking he had lost the plot. "I guess I'd have to see this."

We drove from nearby Calabasas, where we were living at the time, up the winding Old Topanga Canyon road, arriving at a little magical fairyland, with six or seven houses around a big flat green park area. Robert was absolutely right, it was nice, and I could love it as long as I could handle the drive in and out, plus being in the middle of nowhere.

At the end of the road there was a big white house on the right side that was perfect.

"I kind of like this one," I said. "If we live here, we should live in this big white house, because it's right at the end of the cul-de-sac. It looks like it has a huge backyard. It does look quite run down though." The house looked old and in serious disrepair, but it was the best of the bunch.

"Well, that house isn't for sale," Robert pondered, "but if it was, you're absolutely right, it would be perfect. It would be great for kids."

And there was something about this area that felt right. I could envision us living there. We weren't enjoying living in Calabasas in the least. Our gated neighborhood was certainly fancy, but it was excessively quiet and focused on all the wrong values—the right car, the latest fashion, the wealth. Oh, and the Kardashians live there also.

We drove all the way back home, and after the kids were tucked in, we dreamed ourselves to sleep about our big white house in Topanga. The next day we signed up on a few real estate websites for Topanga and tried to forget about the house that wasn't for sale.

Six months later, Robert received an email alert telling us the big white house in Topanga was up for sale.

Radio Heaven.

We made an appointment to view the house and I hated it as soon as I walked in. It needed a lot of work. There was a huge stairwell right in the middle of the house, blocking everything off; the kitchen had a hideous linoleum floor straight out of 1974, which squeaked and stuck to your feet as you walked; and the last update to the fixtures was around the same time. It smelled funny, too.

Robert loved it and wanted to put in an offer that day. I gave myself some time to get used to the idea. Around about this same time, we had started looking at preschools for Jake and Charlie, but were unable to find anything we liked. We were told about a preschool in Topanga called 'Children's Corner' that was natural and earthy and play-based. We fell in love with the school and enrolled Jake who was already old enough to attend. That school was two streets away from the big white house.

Jake's new best friend at school, Piet, lived four doors away from the house. His mother, Hillary, and I became great friends, and she started introducing me to the other women in the neighborhood. I couldn't resist falling in love with the whole neighborhood, the neighbors, and slowly, even the house. We could always remodel, couldn't we?

Our first offer for the house was rejected. The owners were no longer interested in selling and were taking the house off the market. It was confusing and we wanted this house so much. We had already looked at dozens of other houses in Topanga, but couldn't find anything that felt right or didn't have a dangerous plummet at the end of the backyard. A few more months crept by and the owners put the house back on the market again. We put in an offer, they made a counter offer, we put in a new offer, and finally they accepted.

Then the real fun began.

For many reasons repeatedly explained to us by an incredibly patient loan officer, getting a mortgage would prove difficult. First, the bank we applied with was somehow confused by the English system of currency, and with Aspire being based in the U.K. my income and account balances were mystifying and impossible to calculate. Then there were issues

CHAPTER 19 - A LESSON IN RESILIENCE

with the house involving bugs and infestations of all kinds that required immediate treatment.

There was a seemingly endless stream of real estate law and lending jargon foisted upon us, which we were barely able to comprehend. One thing after another, after another, after another for months, which soon became a year and carried on longer still. We had already sold our house in Calabasas and moved into temporary housing in Woodland Hills that, ironically, smelled of curry, taking me back to those early days in Ilford. The months continued to dragged on.

"Sure is taking you a long time to close on this house," people would say. "Are you positive this is the right one?"

"It was meant for us, and we love it!" I would say enthusiastically, but inside, I must admit, I was starting to have my doubts. One day, while driving Jake to pre-school, I gave in to my doubts. This really is taking a long time. Is this the house for us?

I started having a conversation with myself until my head hurt with all the back and forth analysis. I took a deep breath as I wound the car around the curvy Old Topanga Canyon road. And then I came to the spot where the scenery opens up and you catch the majestic and breathtaking Eagle Rock and my doubts dispelled in a moment. This is the place for me, I thought to myself. I knew it was the place. It wasn't the house, it wasn't only the community, the neighborhood, the schools, or the people; it had the perfect combination of everything. I understood in my heart that if we lived there I would be able to make even more of a difference. It would be such a nurturing environment for my family and me, a clear connection.

I said out loud: "If you give me this house, if you make it happen, I promise I will make more of a difference in the world."

I made my deal with the universe. And maybe you're thinking it magically came together, right? Wrong. Really wrong. New issues arose weekly. The bank kept bouncing back paperwork to us. They couldn't understand how my business was based in the U.K. yet I lived in the U.S. They made me source every penny of my income, proving it wasn't drug money smuggled into the country. I had to manually convert every last number from pounds to dollars for the bank and repeatedly educate them on time differences when they kept calling my U.K. accountant in the middle of the night.

A home inspection then revealed the septic system was broken—a huge and expensive issue—and the rest of the house was tired and falling apart. The I.R.S. couldn't issue our returns in time, so every day we called them and tried to hurry the process along to no avail.

All the delays made the owners nervous. They pulled out of our deal and re-listed the house with a different agent, showing it to other people. Thankfully, when nobody else bit, we were back to square one with a new offer for them.

When I said we wanted this house, I meant it.

I remember thinking, I'm not giving up on this house. If something happens, which is completely out of my control, fair enough. But I won't stop trying no matter what if it's in my control. But was this about acknowledging the signs and giving up? Or was it more about persevering despite the obstacles? I was having trouble making the distinction. In the end, the only obstacle that would have stopped me, especially if this house was meant to be ours, was some event that made it completely impossible to obtain. A dead stop. But that never once happened. Were there delays? Yes. Were there mysterious setbacks? Of course. But nothing happened to completely stop us in our tracks.

After spending months in a dreary apartment complex in Woodland Hills with mouse droppings under the kitchen sink and a dead cockroach once falling on my head when I hit the fire alarm with a broom to turn it off, the sale of the big white house was finalized. Closed. DONE.

And it only took three years!

We moved into Topanga. It was an exquisite experience to walk through the front door and relish in the house being ours at last. We were finally home, almost like we had always lived there. The neighbors welcomed us warmly with a string of parties and get-togethers. It was absolutely fantastic. Another dream come true.

A friend of ours named Alberto, an Argentinian scientist turned healer, came over to give us a welcome gift of a Reiki treatment, a system of techniques for healing the body and re-energizing the spirit. During my treatment, I had a powerful vision: a Native American Indian chief stood in the middle of the park in front of our house. He said to me, "Welcome to the neighborhood. I can't protect you from everything that happens or might happen, but I can make sure there are people around to protect you." Topanga is Native American land, so it didn't seem far off, and the image and beautiful message reassured me we were in the right place.

That night we invited some of the neighbors over for gin and tonics under our giant oak tree in our back yard, which became a regular Friday occurrence. I was a little unsure whether to share my Reiki experience with any of my new friends. Off to the side I told Hillary, "I had this Reiki treatment today, and I had this wild vision of a Native American man in the middle of the park."

"You only now saw him?" she said, unfazed. "Did you see the Native American women around him yet?"

I cracked up laughing. We were definitely in the right place if such a story could be trumped with casual ease! We were home. It was wonderful to know there were guides in the park, and we were finally in the right place around like-minded people who cared.

Never underestimate the benefit of being in an environment of like-minded people. It is incredibly powerful. How important it was to know we could be free to say something as wacky as: "Hey, I had this vision of a Native American man!" and the new neighbors being okay with it. Not only did they get it, they had already accepted similar visions.

Resilience is the ability to keep going and bounce back quickly. There will always be aspects of your life and work where you need to keep going, or bounce back. Tune in to why it is critically important you do not give up. What do you need to do more of, or less of, to become more resilient?

Never, ever give up. The key to not giving up, I discovered, is simply not giving up. You must tune into why it is important to carry on and surround yourself with like-minded people who can support and help pick you up when needed.

It was an important lesson for me to learn, and one I was going to rely on again very soon.

CHAPTER 20

Gas & Brakes

Creative visualization refers to the practice of seeking to affect the outer world by changing our internal thoughts and expectations. One of the best known studies on creative visualization compared three groups of Olympic athletes' physical and mental training programs: group one received 100% physical training; group two received 75% physical training with 25% mental training; group three received 50% mental training with 50% physical training. Group three claimed the best performance results, indicating certain types of mental training, such as consciously invoking specific subjective states, can have significant, measurable effects on performance.

Various athletes, business people, and celebrities endorse creative visualization, claiming it has a significant role in their success including Oprah Winfrey, Tiger Woods, Arnold Schwarzenegger, Anthony Robbins, and Bill Gates. In 1987, before he was famous, actor Jim Carey wrote himself a check in the amount of $10 million, he dated it Thanksgiving 1995 and added the notation, "for acting services rendered." He carried the check in his wallet until 1994 when he was paid $10 million for his role in the movie Dumb and Dumber.

As a coach, I was familiar with creative visualization and I used it regularly with my clients to help them formulate goals. It was when we were a few months into living in Topanga that I did a visualization exercise during a training session at a leadership retreat in Northern California. I closed my eyes and traveled to some point in the future when, as I sat in my office at home in a rocking chair, a young woman came to the door and lingered there a few moments, smiling and talking. She wore a long white dress, and she was radiant. She had African skin, hair cut short, a round beaming face, and huge beautiful dark eyes. She was my daughter.

I had gone on this retreat wanting to improve my business skills and came out of it having experienced a personal and rather unexpected vision with a clarity that startled me.

"How was the retreat?" Robert asked the day after I arrived home as we sat at Jerry's Deli on Ventura Boulevard in Woodland Hills for brunch.

I burst into tears. "We have to adopt a little girl from Africa!" I sobbed, realizing instantly I sounded like a nutcase. Jake was four, Charlie nearly three, and Robert about to turn 59. We ran a hectic and frequently stressful household already. Bless Robert! He takes everything in such stride, but this time, he looked at me in nervous shock, nearly swallowing his coffee down the wrong pipe.

"Wh..." he started, knowing I was not only serious, but settled about it. "What?"

I told him all about my vision, concluding my thoughts saying, "But we don't need to do this right now."

As I've already mentioned, Robert is nothing if not wonderful and resilient. He composed himself, and said, "If this is something that you really want and you're passionate about it, then we'll think it through, get our timing right, and do our research. To be sure... because remember," Robert said softly, "you're the gas, I'm the brakes."

A few days later on Skype, I was discussing this adoption idea with Julia who said to me, "Why can't you have your own child? I don't understand why you're adopting since you have two kids of your own."

"I had this visualization," I said realizing how mad it sounded, "and I really want a little girl."

"You can have your own little girl if you want," she said. "You do in vitro fertilization and they can make sure you have a girl." Julia is always connected with the latest ideas, and it sounded intriguing. I investigated a bit and told Robert about my findings. He seemed enthusiastic.

If we could have our own girl, why wouldn't we?

The idea of having our own biological female version of Jake and Charlie was appealing. It was a great idea. We started IVF treatments, quickly realizing that we were the lucky ones; there were many other couples doing IVF with us who were unable to have children at all.

I deeply admire anyone who goes through IVF treatments, because they're not any fun. First, you must inject yourself every day, which means enduring an emotional, mental, and physical roller-coaster of hormonally exaggerated symptoms. It's difficult, it's expensive, it's time consuming, and it's painful, but you do it regardless, you endure all of it for the wonderful little gift that may possibly come into your arms.

For the first couple of weeks of injections, every few days I was required to go to the hospital for a series of invasive procedures to check my progress. The basic premise of IVF is to inject you with a ton of hormones, which stimulate your ovaries and produce tons of eggs to be fertilized. A woman normally produces one egg a month, but I'm nothing if not an achiever—I produced nine.

"You two are doing great. This is going to be a breeze," the doctor said to us on the day the eggs were fertilized.

"Yes," we agreed. After all, I had gotten pregnant quickly with Jake and Charlie. This would be a no-brainer, and the only reason we were doing it was for our guaranteed girl. Some people do IVF five, six, seven times and nothing happens. Many couples go through years of expense, heartbreak and torture to no avail, fixated by the story of 'that woman' who gave birth at 49-years old, but not us. Our eggs were fertilized and growing well and it would just take a few days in the Petri dish. After that, I'd return to the hospital, be injected with the now fertilized, female eggs. I would get pregnant and have my baby girl. Job done. It would be easy. I walked by the childless couples in the waiting room like an alien. Hi, I'm only here because I want a guaranteed girl.

Every day of the process we were told everything was fine. The eggs were growing well, and out of nine there were five good ones, an unusually high number, and before implanting, they would already have it figured out which were girls and which boys. All was going swimmingly.

I decided to call my baby girl Grace. The 'G' standing for Gillian, after my mum, was fulfilling a Jewish tradition to take the first letter from a special family member's name. The name Grace represented beauty, calm, peace, and a regal elegance to me. I loved the name, and settled on calling her Grace.

Emma would say to me, "Don't worry, Sam, Grace is coming soon," and when I used to go on my walks around Topanga to exercise during the grueling IVF, I would listen on my iPod to the song Amazing Grace.

Amazing Grace, how sweet the sound,

That saved a wretch like me.

I once was lost but now am found,

Was blind, but now I see.

When the day came to go in for the transplant, we were both so excited. That Sunday morning we asked Jay to look after the boys, and we were about to walk out the door when the phone rang. I picked up the call on the phone in the bedroom, put it on speaker and gestured Robert into the room. It was the doctor from the clinic.

"Sam?" he said. "I'm afraid I don't have good news."

"What is it?" I said. I felt my body slump onto the bed.

"I'm so sorry," he said. "We received your test results back and all five eggs are deformed. We won't be able to do your procedure today."

"I don't understand."

He repeated himself. It was over. The IVF didn't work for us, either. Instantly, we were that couple. I hung up the phone and slumped onto the bed. Robert and I both burst into tears. Robert, now quite attached to the idea, cried so intensely it surprised me. As weird as it may sound, we cried like we had lost five babies.

It was only 9 a.m., so we asked Jay to stay with the boys as planned. We drove down to the ocean to clear our heads, along Pacific Coast Highway to Malibu's Paradise Cove restaurant. Robert ordered some breakfast and a Mimosa. I drank a couple too. I hadn't drunk during IVF and I wanted to deaden the pain. I was so confused—there was the Radio Heaven vision, and an extremely strong gut feeling, knowing we were going to have a girl. I didn't understand what was happening. It felt like the biggest possible F-you from the universe. It didn't make sense to me, why we were being halted this way. Was I to take it up as another challenge, go through another round of IVF, and jump on another emotional roller coaster? Did I have the courage? Could we afford it?

Was this another challenge like buying the house?

"We should try again," Robert said. "It doesn't often work the first time, like they said."

But something inside me said a quiet, "No." We'd taken a wrong turn, gone almost all the way, but were dramatically halted. We were tempted by something not meant to be, and we needed to be reminded why we were doing this in the first place.

"No, Robert." I said. "Do you remember the vision?" The alarm bell sounded off in both our heads. Tuned in to Radio Heaven at last!

"Adopt," Robert said, knowing before he'd even spoken.

Having our own baby seemed right, or normal; like the logical, rational, more secure choice. But what did having our own baby really mean? We didn't make any final decisions that day, we needed some time to think. In the two weeks following the failure of the IVF, I was depressed. I cried easily and often. Robert was chin-up, but faking it, taking on most of the work with the boys. One day I caught him crying in the garage.

"Something good is happening here," Robert said, to encourage me, yes, but also because he knew it was true. "We're going to find out what it is soon."

But I couldn't see the good. I didn't understand this one. As optimistic and encouraging as Robert could be, he was also desperately sad, and doing an equal amount of soul-searching. It felt like a slap in the face. In fact, it was a slap in the face, but we didn't get the message, not for another two weeks.

We were driving up Old Topanga Canyon Road, on our way home from buying groceries, with Jake and Charlie sitting in their car seats in the back seat. It came to me as Robert drove through the bends on the high mountain road. First, there was the timing: we were trying to speed it up on our own. Then, we were shown the plan and ignored it; we were meant to have a daughter, and she would come from somewhere far away, some other way, and it was not up to us how.

"I don't want to do IVF again," as I spoke the words, a wave of relief swept over me like an ocean breeze. I hadn't said much in the past weeks and it felt suddenly liberating to give voice to my distaste. I hated doing IVF, but felt like I should if I was able to, but I had already dealt with my shoulds a long time ago.

"Okay," said Robert, resolved. He knew it too. I love my husband— no debate, pure unconditional support and love. "Okay," he said again, putting it away once and for all.

"We're off track. We were meant to adopt," I said. "The only thing about adopting that bothers me is how can we know we'll really love and bond with a child that's not born to us?" I cringed as I spoke the words. That's the most ridiculous thing that could possibly come out of your mouth, Sam! Of course we would love her; it was our destiny, it was meant to be and she was meant to be ours. It wasn't that adoption was a last resort because we couldn't have a biological child; instead, adoption was what we were supposed to try first.

"Then we'll adopt," Robert said. "Maybe we should adopt from Russia, that's both our family heritage. Then she'll look like Jake and Charlie. That would be good."

I thought about it for a moment, and said, "Would it be good, really? I don't know. Do we really need to have our family all looking alike?"

Robert said, "Well, I suppose if we're going to adopt, we should be a little more open about it."

"I agree, but I don't think she's coming from Russia," I said. "In my vision, she was black. So most likely she's coming from Africa. Wouldn't it be something to make a real difference to a child there? And maybe it's important for Jake and Charlie to understand not everyone in the world has what they have. It could be enlightening for them, too. People may stare at our family, since it doesn't look right, but it's a strong statement that diversity in gender and culture is good for everyone!"

Robert was quiet as we pulled onto our driveway. "Let's get the kids in," he said.

Later that evening, as we were having dinner, Robert said, "You know, I've been thinking about what you said. I like the idea. I mean, I really like the idea, it feels right."

I started researching adoption the next day. We were back in the groove. Over the next few weeks, the Democratic Republic of Congo kept appearing on my web searches and e-mails. Whenever the DRC popped up in my inbox, I would think, "I hope it won't be there. It's too scary.

I don't want to go there." This is a country at war almost perpetually since 1998; a place where the weapons of warfare are rape and sexual violence against women and girls. A devastated country I was aware of though my coaching work with Women for Women International. I had even glued a picture of women survivors of war from the DRC who had become community leaders on my latest vision board in my office. I felt a connection to this country, but at the same time, a great fear of having to go there to adopt a child.

In any case, wherever Robert and I were adopting from, we would want to retain some link with the country. I would never want my adopted daughter coming to me in twenty years saying, "What do you know about the country I was born in?" And have to say, "Well, nothing, honey, we've never visited there and we didn't really think you'd care after this many years."

I'm slow sometimes, but I'm not completely dense; I had practically asked for the DRC to be in my life. So, one day when I was sitting in front of my laptop in my home office, I closed my eyes for a moment and I tried to connect to our little girl. I said, "Are you in the Democratic Republic of Congo?"

"Yes, I am."

Radio Heaven.

"Shit. Okay, so it's the DRC then! Fair enough, Grace."

I stopped looking anywhere else. It was a done deal. Grace was in the DRC, one of the most dangerous countries for women in the world. It was going to happen. I knew she was there. I threw myself into full research mode. Within the adoption community, so many caring people reached out to help and over Christmas 2012, while Julia was out visiting us from England, we spoke to many families who had adopted children from the DRC. As I gathered information and connected with them, the picture improved dramatically. I was finally ready to let Robert know that our daughter would most likely be coming from the DRC.

So in January 2013, a few months before I started writing this book, we settled on adopting a little girl from the Democratic Republic of Congo and began the process. A few weeks later, a new client from Chicago approached Robert and, as it turned out, he happened to be from the DRC. Robert had never before had a client from anywhere in Africa. We started getting e-mails about contributing towards the funds for women in the DRC. Where was this coming from? Then I received an email from Women for Women International saying, "We're hosting a run for International Women's Day in Regent's Park in London in March. It's a 10K. Would you be interested?"

"Well, I'm not sure," I said. "I'm not really a runner since having kids. Who's the aid for?"

"Women in Congo."

"I'll do it." No question.

I was out of running shape, and ran out of breath going around the block, as I hadn't exercised at all during the IVF. I didn't know if I was capable of running a 10K. So I ran to Red Rock trail, about a half-mile away from our house—if I could make it to the park, I could try pushing further. But I didn't make it to the park, in fact, I stopped, panting and exhausted about half way there. Dejected and feeling fat, I walked home, plopped down, and ate cookies.

The 10K was only four weeks away, so I asked my old personal trainer, Mike, to help me train. I needed support. Mike doesn't like to run, he is more of a weights man, so I don't think he was too keen but he rode his bike next to me as I ran. It was mostly early mornings, so we didn't talk much, but he's a total bastard when it comes to training, and doesn't take any moans or excuses.

Get on with it.

Soon we built up so I could make it to the park. It would take me roughly eight round trips from my house to the park entrance to reach my target of 10K. Mike pushed me even harder. And, slowly but surely,

I actually did run 10K, back and forth from my own home. It was tremendously hard for me to achieve, but my little trick when it was difficult toward the end of the run was to imagine little Grace playing with her brothers, Jake and Charlie, out in the green park area in front of our house. That picture helped me through every time.

When I arrived in London, I was ready for the Regents Park run. Julia ran with me, my ever faithful high-achiever. Gillian came to watch, along with Emma, her best-friend Verity, my niece Serena and nephew Samuel.

Race day was a classic spring morning in London and the air was crisp and cold as hundreds of other runners were gathered for their marathon qualifier, along with the handful of us running for Congo Women. Verity was a seasoned marathon runner and told us what to do and where to go.

We took off for three laps around Regents Park. The marathon runners sprinted, while we jogged and chatted. Wow! This would be easy-breezy after Mike's training me in 100-degree heat, over rocks and stones and up the Red Rock Topanga trails. This is a piece of cake. I'll do this again... maybe a marathon!

After two times around the park, all the marathon qualifiers had finished and it was only us running for our Congo friends. One final time around and I'd be down at the pub for Sunday lunch and a beer with Gillian and Emma. Suddenly, a searing pain shot down my right side, a stabbing runner's side stitch. "Run through a stitch!" I could hear Mike hollering. I kept running, determined not to walk, having promised myself I wouldn't walk any of it, I would keep running no matter what.

That pesky little voice chimed in: "Stop for a second, Sam. Catch your breath, you've done well, it's fine to walk a while." I slowed down and stumbled along, the stitch was bad from that combination of severe jet lag and the banana I'd wolfed down before the race. A woman I'd passed earlier, gained on me and asked if I was doing okay.

"Yes," I squeaked. There was a moment when I hated myself for doing this. I was tempted to give up, but then, at last, I saw the finish line, about 300-yards out. One woman running past me waved to her cheering husband and sons, making me wish Robert and the boys were there.

"You've done your best"

"It's not smart to run in pain"

"Everyone will understand why you didn't finish"

"You could walk the last little bit and that would be fine"

I kept running, trying to evoke all the physical energy I could muster. It wasn't working. I felt like I was going to throw up, but I stumbled on. My right knee, hurt during training, felt like it was about to buckle. I chanted in my head: "running for Congo women, running for Congo women." I tried to imagine being a woman in Congo, and how I should be able to get through a bloody 10K race if they can survive the atrocities of war they endure daily. Get a grip, Sam. Then it came to me: If my daughter can be alive right now in the Democratic Republic of Congo, I can damn well run this race. If Grace can do that, then I can be here, and do this.

Then I hear it, somehow, her voice saying, "Come on, Mama! You can do it!"

Radio Heaven.

I can't explain it—and yes, I know she can't even speak English—but Grace helped me through the last leg of the race, when I was so close to giving up. I actually sped up and sprinted the final 200 yards into the finish line with a respectable time of 1:03. It proved to me that we can go beyond certain physical and mental limits when we tune in to Radio Heaven's bigger purpose.

In this way, when the going gets tough, you can tune into a greater purpose for the help you may need. Finding a way of regularly quieting your mind, whether you simply close your eyes and focus on deepening your breath, or you practice meditation, yoga, or an exercise of some kind, it is a non-negotiable necessity to create space in your everyday life, and tune back in to your visions for the future. Have a moment to ask yourself powerful questions while your mind is quiet: What do I need to do now? What is most important for me to know?

My temporary side-stitch was minuscule compared to what my daughter-to-be had already been through. The entire experience, from the initial visualization of Grace, to the IVF treatments, and coming full-circle back to the original vision, made me understand the importance of staying on course even when distractions and obstacles attempt to throw me off and make me want to stop.

Thank you, Grace. I ran this race for you, for your mother, and for all the wonderful women in the DR Congo that are like her.

CHAPTER 21

The Journey to Grace

The global charity UNICEF estimates 153 million children worldwide, ranging from infants to teenagers, have lost one or both parents. Many of these children live in orphanages or die on the streets. One answer is adoption, but adoptions have fallen by more than 60% since 2004, due in large part to a broken system filled with delays, bureaucracy, discrimination, and staggering costs incurred by adoptive parents. UNICEF also estimates 15% of the Democratic Republic of Congo's under-18 population, roughly 5 million children, are orphans as a result of a civil war spanning decades, which claims the lives of one child out of seven before they can reach just five years old.

It was July 16, 2013—a Tuesday, to be exact. It had been six months since we had started the adoption process and I was right in the heart of the City of London on one of my U.K. visits. Robert and I settled on me going back to the U.K. on my own four times a year for about a week each visit. Robert stayed with the kids in California, and with Jay's help, they were doing well. I could work and visit Emma at the same time. My sister had become a successful pediatric nurse living in Poole, on the south coast with her husband and four children.

It had been a fantastic day. After wrapping up an Aspire event titled 'Raising Your Profile,' led with my right-hand woman, Carolyn Dawson, fifty remarkable women stayed behind for a couple of drinks and networking. At about 8.30 p.m. I headed back to the Zetter hotel. I was happily exhausted and getting ready for bed when I called Robert at home in California to check on him and the kids and say goodnight.

"Did you receive the email?" Robert said.

"What email?"

"There's an email in your inbox from our adoption agency. You must have seen it by now."

I scanned through my email quickly. "No, nothing."

"Well, check in your deleted folder or your junk folder, maybe it is in there by accident?"

"I still don't see it."

"Well", he says, "You have to see this email because it's about a little girl up for adoption. It wasn't specifically sent to us as an option because she is four, maybe five, and we asked for a two year old, but I think you should see this email. I'll forward it to you."

The email pinged into my inbox.

Subject: Need a home for a waiting child

Message: Please pass the word. This girl is at our Arms of Love Orphanage and is about five years old. There is very little background on this child. I am sorry we had to shave her hair. There were lice when this group of children came in. She is 41 inches tall, so that is 50% for age four, but since most of the children are malnourished, we added a year to be on the safe side.

Attached was a photo of a little girl with huge eyes and a little half smile. Her eyes were so big, like two deep pools of hope. She was holding a placard in front of her, which I didn't register initially, because I was completely immersed in her eyes, as if she were looking right into me and saying, "Mama, here I am. I'm waiting for you."

My eyes flooded with tears of joy, relief, calm, peace, and excitement all at the same time.

"There's our girl," I whispered. "Oh, wow. There's our Grace." I was in love, instantly and undeniably. It was exactly like the moments when I gave birth to Jake and Charlie, when I held them in my arms—I could have walked across the earth and back for them. I had read somewhere how this can happen when you adopt; when you see that first picture and you somehow know. To tell you the truth, I thought the story was a bit of adoption folklore. How could it possibly happen with a photo? But, it happened that day to me, and I knew, somehow, that she was our Grace.

Radio Heaven was playing our song!

I sat on the bed in my hotel room, still dolled up in business attire and make-up, on the phone with Robert, tears streaming down my face. As I was having my stars-crossing-moons moment, I could hear Robert talking away on the phone. His words became coherent again and he was saying something about the placard and wasn't it so cool?

"The what?" I said, finally conscious.

From time to time, as we were going through the adoption process, I thought about her name. Many adopted children have their names changed: Yin from China becomes Amy and Sevi from Africa becomes Susan. Sometimes their original name becomes their middle or second name. The typical advice is the older they are, the more their name is linked to their identities, and enough change is taking place without changing their name, too. I battled with it a bit. Would I change her name? I so wanted my Grace. Our family and friends already knew the story and were calling her Grace long before we knew who she was or where she was from.

"I said look at her name placard," Robert repeated.

Her actual real name is Grace? Are you joking?

If ever there was a Radio Heaven moment in my life, where time stood still and my heart thumped inside my chest, this was it. I may have actually heard angels singing! It was such a confirmation, although I needed none, but there it was. This was our Grace. Wonder and satisfaction swept over me, like all the stars, moons and everything else in the universe aligned at this perfect point, at this perfect time. Grace's big brown eyes looked back at me and I knew.

Still, Robert is a practical man. "Sam," he said, "don't fall in love yet, just because her name is Grace. She still may not be the one."

I was grateful we were on the phone because tears were streaming down my face, which was now all red and puffy, and my body shook with astonishment. "Yes," I said, a fresh tear coursing down my face, "of course," and another, "I know we mustn't get too... and we need to really make sure," the tears were really running out now, "everything is correct and check she is the one we're looking for." I strained to remain as practical as I could, to make sure Robert had what he needed, too. But inside, a rebellion brewed—and a little sadness. Robert wasn't having the intuitive hit that I was. Could I be wrong? I started internally stamping my feet. How could he not see her? I am hating the fact you don't see her, Robert! I felt anger toward him that I had never known before.

He carried on calmly, and I forced myself to listen.

"It's that she is a little older than what we were thinking," he said. "We really need to think this through."

"Yes, okay." I said. "Let's think through what we need to think through then." He caught the edge in my voice.

"Well, I want to call the adoption agency," he said, "to check the girl's medical details and find out her situation and then I'll call you back."

Wait. Did he call her the girl? And what's to check? I grit my teeth. I already know she is right for us, and we're ready for her, why the hell don't you? At that moment, I was grateful to be on the phone and 5,000 miles away, otherwise a major argument might have ensued.

We said goodnight. I took a shower and laid down on the bed, sleepless, ecstatic and thinking all night about our little Grace; seeing her face, looking into her eyes on the photo, wondering about the life ahead of her. Any resentment toward Robert's pesky sensibleness started to evaporate as I imagined he and the boys embracing her fully. Robert would realize we had finally found her, the daughter we had been searching for. Or, had she found us?

It was 2 a.m., then 3 a.m., then 4 a.m. She's an hour ahead of me right now in Congo, I thought. Is she awake with me? Could she know, too, somehow? My alarm rang at 6 a.m., I had had barely two hours of sleep and was due to speak to a few hundred high-flying women of London at the new City Mother's Network in Canary Wharf at lunchtime.

As I prepared for my talk, it felt a lot like those first days of falling in love with Robert all over again. I was filled with feelings of excitement and joy, and my tunnel-vision was making it difficult for me to concentrate. Grace encompassed every thought of my mind. In the taxi, on my way to Canary Wharf, I shared the news with the cab driver.

"What happened to her real parents?" he asked.

Her real parents? Like we were not going to be her real parents? I was a little stunned, I couldn't answer that question. Wow, that is probably a question I'm going to have to answer a lot over the course of my life, and so will Grace.

When the taxi dropped me off, I found myself staring at a huge, brand new, glass building in Canary Wharf, which must have been over 40-floors tall. It belonged to one of the leading laws firms in the world and contained their newly built flagship offices. Briefly, old fears reared up: Who was I to be speaking here today? What if they had it wrong? What if they don't like me? Well, if they didn't like me there was no way to tell, because not only did they let me into their nice building, they gave me an escort up in the elevator and led me to a beautiful glass room with a panoramic view of London. I glugged down a cup of coffee, found the restroom, and assumed the position in the usual spot for a quick mediation—toilet, lid down.

With my fears calmed, I put a few drops into my reddened, sleep-deprived eyes. Time to get to work. I've got this.

During my talk I shared my vision board story and how I met Robert. I looked out at the smiling faces of these wonderful women, mothers like me, tired like me, anxious about balancing work and life like me and I could bet a good handful of them didn't get much sleep last night either.

The women who work in the financial district of London are arguably some of the smartest women on the planet: lawyers, bankers, and accountants working in one of the last bastions of male culture. To be successful in this city is one of the toughest accomplishments a person can achieve, and to achieve it as a woman is even more difficult, but to achieve it as a mother, well, that is extraordinary.

I am in awe of them. I can see their ambition, their drive, their toughness—but I also see their vulnerability, their nurturing, their motherliness. It doesn't matter whether a woman has children or not, it is her nature to care and nurture, to fight for the ones she loves, like mothers do. The teams they manage, the boards they convene, and the clients they have won should be so grateful to have these women as part of their lives.

There we were, enjoying each other's company near the top of this modern building with food fit for a royal banquet and in the heart of one of the most affluent areas of planet earth. What is wrong with this picture?

Something signaled inside of me. I remembered the mothers all over the world, suffering and barely making enough to feed their children; so many mothers like Grace's mother, who recognize the only salvation for their children, for having a better life, is to give them up, or abandon them. So I told these London women about The Aspire Foundation, about our mentoring program, how they could become a mentor and change the life of a woman in need, and very likely save the lives of many. One woman put up her hand.

"Yes?I said.

"I'm one of your mentors," she said, and she stood to see the crowd.

I took an expectant breath.

"I want to tell everyone here," she continued, "about what a fantastic experience it has been. You should all definitely consider this."

What a testimonial! That's how women can be, word of mouth counting much more than anything else. As my 30-minute presentation came to an end, despite my lack of sleep, I successfully delivered my presentation and the response was positive. I made some new friends, some new clients, but something still seemed wrong. What had I left out?

Grace.

"But it's not 100% yet," the little voice said, "Robert hasn't called you back, he's fact-finding and you should wait." Again, if there is one thing about should, it's that it brings out the fighter in me. The day I do what I should will be a sad day indeed.

Fuck it, I thought, like I'm flying an F-18 fighter jet, I'm going in! What better a place to make the announcement about Grace, than to my wonderful City Mothers? Since I was officially finished with my presentation, the women were already starting to get up, milling about and chatting. "I have an announcement to make," I said into the microphone. The crowd hushed, everyone looking at me quizzically, a tad anxious for the gorgeous banquet, and one woman later told me they thought I was about to sell them something. "I gave birth today!" The words zipped out without thought or hesitation. Until that moment, I had never before seen a few hundred high-flying women of London do a collective double take.

Has she gone completely mad? All my credibility started to flag.

"I look good on it, don't I?" I received a nervous laugh there, restoring some confidence within the group. "You see, my husband and I have wanted to adopt a little girl for a long while, and last night we found out who she is." They all burst into smiles and applause. I continued the story about how I had decided many years ago to give my daughter, whoever she might be, the name Grace. It was a nice moment.

"Would you like to see a picture of her?"

"Yes!" they said in unison.

The tech-guy did his thing with my laptop and up on the 10-foot screen she went.

"Awwwww..." they said around the room, enthralled by those two big deep pools of hope looking out at them. They, too, had not yet noticed the placard board with her name written on it.

"Look at her real name placard."

The room fell silent.

I looked out and saw some women crying. They weren't crying for me, or for Grace, but for the confirmation that good things do happen that we sometimes can't reasonably explain. But these highly analytical and highly intelligent women recognized that something greater is out there providing for us, protecting us, and helping us when we think big and are resilient, and that the world is, in fact, a good place.

I call it Radio Heaven.

They started clapping like crazy, tears were streaming down our beautifully made-up faces, and I was met with a standing ovation. It was a phenomenal moment to let other mothers know about you, Grace, and to celebrate with them and have a wonderful time. So many women came up to me at the end and said how they laughed and cried and were happy for me and for Grace and for our growing family. They were grateful for the story inspiring them to make a bigger difference in their life, their work, and their world.

I returned to my hotel on a major high. After two days of great events and finding out about Grace and the confirming reaction from City Mothers, I came back to my hotel to do what I always do when I get back into my room, wherever I am in the world. I sat on my bed and phoned Robert.

I was ready to spill the whole blow-by-blow account of my day, but something was wrong—Robert was too somber. "Sam, I've found some information out about Grace and need to share some issues with you," he said. He sounded rehearsed and cautious. This wasn't going to be good. My face flushed, my breathing quickened, and my chest tightened. I sat down heavily on the bed kicking my heels off on the floor.

"Sam," he repeated, "we've been advised to not adopt Grace."

My happy heart stopped beating.

"What do you mean advised? What happened?"

"Well, mainly," he said, "she's slightly older than we really should take." Robert spoke in a measured, monotone voice, fading in and out, choosing his words carefully and trying to not upset me. "It's her age. She's five months younger than Jake and ten months older than Charlie. The experts told me they think it's not good since she's in the middle. It's not going to work. I'm sorry, Sam, but I don't think we should take her."

I was stunned. He sounded so sure.

"That's what the experts said," he said again.

"Who are the experts?"

"The adoption agency," he said, "that's what they advised. They said they've had trouble with this kind of thing before. The kids are too close in age, Jake and Grace are going to be in the same year at school and it creates too much competition. What if she came all the way out here and it didn't work out?"

Radio Heaven signs aside, I do love my husband and I trust his judgment. I also trusted the judgment of our adoption agency. The situation was analyzed, compared against similar scenarios, a reasoned assessment was made, and it was time to move on. But I was baffled, and my circuits were on overload. My head was saying we needed to move on, but in my heart, how on earth could I be so completely wrong? Did I only want this Grace because I saw her name and blindly followed omens? Did I let myself get too carried away?

I suddenly felt foolish for making the announcement at City Mothers. What would I say if I met those women again? "Yes, sorry, it was all a mix up, we never did adopt that girl..." God, would I actually say that girl? And they would say, "Oh, that's too bad," but, in fact, would be thinking, Yes, well, we did think it was all a bit far-fetched. Too good to be true, you know, the thing with her name and all.

But once I stopped questioning, something started to brew; this snap judgment was totally wrong. From a very deep, very gut level, I was sure I was right about Grace, but I had nothing to back me up, nothing Robert could believe or hang on to. Then I was immediately angry with Robert, absolutely livid. How could he listen to this agency person and not his heart? Had he not seen her photo? Had he not registered her name, looked into her face and loved her? I trusted him, didn't he trust me?

It started to get heated on the phone. At first, we disagreed. Then, we strongly disagreed. Then, we vehemently disagreed. He seemed sad, but he was resigned, mind made up. For him it was all over. For me—well, I would have to call him back later. I said so, and put the phone down.

It was 8 p.m. by then, a rare beautiful summer evening in England and still light outside. I needed to get out of my hotel room, so I glugged down a room service wine and scrambled outside. I needed some space, some air. I needed to breathe and I needed to think and I needed to connect. Out on the street, London buzzed with people outside the pubs and restaurants drinking, smoking, and eating. I walked, getting a few strange looks at my business dress, with the casual shoes, and runny mascara covered eyes. I walked further, hearing the same thing in my mind, over and over again: You have to fight for her. I kept walking, and the thought occurred to me to get on a plane to the Congo right then, look her in the eyes in person, and then come back and tell Robert I knew she was our child. He would have to believe me if I saw her face to face. Could that be the answer?

No.

This must be won with intellect and practicality, I had to find a way to prove it right. I would have a fight on my hands, not against Robert or the adoption agency, but against whatever was preventing us from being together with our daughter Grace. Not an emotional fight, a real honest to goodness council estate-style brawl.

I rushed back to the hotel room, more calm, readied and sobered. Robert had one expert. I needed an expert, too. I emailed our social worker Diana, back in Los Angeles. I explained the situation and asked her opinion. "You know us. You've come to our home. You've met our children. You've given us in depth interviews. You've approved us for adoption. So what do you think? You're an expert as much as any of these other people, will this actually work?"

She was in California and I was in England, an 8-hour time difference, but she emailed back right away with: "I know there are varying thoughts regarding birth order; however, as all the kids are so young and your referral is of different gender then I do not believe birth order is a big factor. Especially, if you feel a strong connection."

Yes, pretty strong connection here.

I sent the email on to Robert immediately. Score 1-1, and I was going for one more point, for the win. Diana gave us another recommendation: as soon as we received any referral, we should immediately contact Dr. Gary Feldman, an international adoption expert who looks at all of the information to give an opinion on whether it is a good match or not. He is almost always right, Diana says.

Step one: Email Gary Feldman. Check. Sent in two minutes.

Step two: Arrange a conference call. Check. He was available Friday and would confirm the time.

Step three: Get Robert in on that call with us. Check.

Friday was two days away. I couldn't speak to Robert that night, I just couldn't. It was the next day when he and I finally spoke. We had both calmed down by then, and I was reassured by the relief Robert expressed reading the social worker's email.

We waited anxiously for Friday, which was the last day of my trip and the day I reserved for my London friends: Gillian, Julia, and Nis. It was the end of a long week and I definitely needed to relax and wind down with my girls.

Gillian and Julia, two of my oldest friends, are very different from each other. Gillian is introspective and deeply cynical with a sarcastic sense of humor, while Julia has about four-million friends and loves a good party. Nis, the newest member of our group, is sassy and smart and was then about to leave her big banking job to start a business helping goddess women, quite a bit of career change.

It all felt very Sex and The City.

We met at the Sanctuary Spa in Covent Garden, and sprawled out on the large beds and lounge chairs by the koi pond, catching up on all the news, giggling and drinking champagne. Although it's not allowed, I stashed my cell phone in my robe pocket, checking text messages regularly, awaiting Robert to confirm the time for the teleconference with Dr. Feldman.

Julia was a little mad with me, saying, "Why do you keep checking your phone, Sam?"

I spilled the beans, telling them everything that had happened. They were wildly supportive of my upcoming battle. That's what's great about good friends, whatever I said, I knew they would stick by my side, but that text was taking a long time. Finally, at 8:25 p.m., my phone buzzed in my robe.

The text: Con call 9pm UK. Luv u.

The text had been delayed by a few hours because of the weak signal in the spa.

Shit.

Here we sat in robes and wet hair, no place at the spa to have a quiet call, not to mention we've also drunk quite a lot of bubbly. Where can I do this call? Panic starts to set in. But Julia, as ever the organizer and problem solver of any group, started to quick-march everyone.

"No time for showers," Julia said. "Everyone get dressed, let's pay the bill and go to my house." Julia's house wasn't far. She had a gorgeous flat opposite the swanky Sanderson hotel off Oxford Street in the heart of London's W1.

We had our orders. Throwing on our clothes, no shower, soggy hair, and a bit tipsy. It was an interesting scene as we all exited one by one into a busy Friday night in Covent Garden. Julia, who knows London like the back of her hand and, like myself, is one who cannot be swayed by any argument when she's sure, announced as we left the spa that trying to get a taxi would be useless at this time on a Friday night and that we all should run. She gave us precise details of how had done this run before and it would take 14 minutes.

I began to worry as it was already 8:44 p.m. by my watch. I pictured Robert's disapproving face—Oh, this is so important to you and you're not ready?

So, we ran. It was a Friday night in Leicester Square and the streets were teeming with people. Nis was our cheerleader, encouraging us all forward, and Gillian, ever the H.R. Director, made sure we made it across traffic safely, even leaving herself on the other side of the road when the traffic light changed to green unexpectedly. The rest of us on the other side of the traffic saw Gillian raise her arm, and she shouted dramatically across to us like she was about to bleed out in some old war-movie scene, "Go! Go on without me!" I laughed so hard, I nearly fell over but we waited for her—never leave your sister in arms behind—as she dodged traffic to get over to the other side of the road with us.

Julia soared on ahead, and what a sight! Six-feet of gorgeous legs, blond wet hair, and big boobs on a mission, zooming across the London streets. Men turned their heads as though magnetized, all normal behavior for men around Julia. I kept checking my phone as the minutes counted down. We were now running at top speed, or as top speed as you can go in high heels, yelling out the countdown: "We've five minutes everybody!" "Now we've four minutes!" "Three minutes left!" "Oh God, one minute, hurry, Sam!"

Thirty seconds before 9:00 p.m. we opened the red door to Julia's swanky W1 ground floor flat.

I'm not late!

I ran downstairs to use the phone in her bedroom and Julia ran after me, pushing a pad and pen into my hand. I took a deep breath, gulped down water from the glass shoved in front of me by Gillian, and dialed the number as I sat with Nis patting my shoulder. Robert and Gary were already on the call, chatting calmly.

"There she is," said Robert, happily, ever proud of his wife.

"Sorry to be a little late gentlemen," I say all businesslike; little do they know. "Shall we get started?" Inside, of course, I'm repeating today's mantra: Please, Dr. Gary Feldman, tell us this is a good referral!

"I've reviewed all of Grace's medical details," Gary said, "and all of her documents. And all I can say is this is a great referral. We have all good information on her. She looks healthy. I would say it all looks great."

Not much of a fight, that!

Relief flooded in on both Robert and me. Only he was delighted on two fronts: that Grace was ours, and that he wouldn't need to argue it with his wife. Robert and I asked Gary about fifty questions each. Do you think there are any issues? Do you think her age is an issue and the fact that she is going to be in the middle of our two boys? One question after another, he put our concerns to rest. He was calm and practical. What a relief! I heard Robert sigh and sensed his relief, too. Sure, I needed to find another expert, but not any old expert, this guy was top of his field. He bombarded us with scientific data, his experience, his analysis of her paperwork and photos, and his professional opinion. A magic combination of strong gut feelings, backed up by data and expertise. Unbeatable!

We said goodnight to Dr. Feldman, but Robert and I stayed on the line together; ecstatic doesn't come close to describing our feelings. My strategy worked, and it was a nice win. Robert sounded relieved and we were again right in step with each other. I believed in Radio Heaven more strongly than ever before. We wanted a daughter, and we found her, she was called Grace, and now she would arrived to complete our family.

Grace, you are coming home!

Big dreams can actually come true and you, too, can find your grace. It takes guts, resilience and there will be obstacles to overcome to make your dreams a reality. Just remember how important it is to be extraordinarily clear about what you want and why you want it. Sometimes our loved ones present the biggest challenges and we have to find convincing combinations of both emotional and logical arguments to prove our case. Enlisting other opinions or neutral perspectives can help build both the head and heart elements of our case.

Ultimately, I have learned to tune into Radio Heaven and listen to the signs it presents along the way that keep me on track. I found Grace and she is the elegance, beauty, and mercy of my life-journey thus far. And that keeps me going no matter what.

As you read this book, I find myself imagining what your next step is. I hope that you have been inspired to make your own dreams a reality. Take a moment now to turn on the radio and tune into your message from Radio Heaven. It's time for you to listen to your gut feelings, and those seemingly random songs and coincidental lyrics—if you will listen with your heart, they will lead you to your own journey to grace.

ABOUT THE AUTHOR

Dr. Sam Collins was named "One of the Top 200 Women to Impact Business & Industry" by Her Majesty, The Queen of England and was named as "One of the Top 10 Coaches in the UK" by The Sunday Times. She is also the winner of the Ogunte Women's Social Leadership Award in the category of Leader in the Workplace. Her Ph.D. explored the future world of work for women as leaders in the U.S. and the U.K.

Sam is an inspirational speaker and coach who believes in the power of women to change business and the world at large. She creates and leads conferences, events, and workshops. She has worked with women leaders from more than 50 countries over the past 20 years and has contributed to The Financial Times, CNN, The Sunday Times and the BBC Global Business Report.

Originally from London, UK, Sam now lives in Southern California with her husband, two sons, and daughter.

Printed in Great Britain
by Amazon

67617091R00122